Praise for *A Tale of Two Soldiers*

"The American soldier Max Gendelman's story of his six-decades long friendly relationship with the German pilot Karl Kirschner gives a rare glimpse not only of the personal toll of WWII but also of the triumph of personal friendship against improbable odds."

—Klaus Scharioth, former German Ambassador to the U.S., 2006-2011

"A fascinating and inexplicable story about an American POW and a German officer that will move readers even as they learn about the hardships that American soldiers endured."

—Deborah E. Lipstadt, author of *The Eichmann Trial*

"This World War II memoir is a remarkable history of survival and friendship. If an American military sniper—a young Jewish man from Milwaukee—can befriend a German Luftwaffe pilot and become lifelong friends, then we can all certainly hope for a better world."

—Wolf Blitzer, CNN

"This is truly a love story, and a grand tale of courage, faith, honor and most importantly, friendship. It is also the story of bigotry, and the injustices of anti-Semitism. May their memories be for a blessing."

—Hannah Rosenthal, Special Envoy to Monitor and Combat Anti-Semitism under the Obama Administration, 2009-2012

A TALE
OF
TWO
SOLDIERS

A TALE
OF
TWO
SOLDIERS

THE UNEXPECTED FRIENDSHIP BETWEEN
A WWII AMERICAN JEWISH SNIPER AND
A GERMAN MILITARY PILOT

MAX GENDELMAN

TWO HARBORS PRESS, MINNEAPOLIS

Two Harbors Press
322 1ˢᵗ Avenue North, Suite 500
Minneapolis, MN 55401
612.455.2293
www.TwoHarborsPress.com

ISBN-13: 978-1-62652-288-6
LCCN: 2013913472

Gendelman, Max
1. World War, 1939-1945--Prisoners and prisons. 2. World War, 1939-1945--Personal Narratives. 3. German Prisoners of War--Germany--Biography. 4. American Anti-Semitism. 5. Gendelman, Max, 1923-2012. 6. Kirschner, Karl, 1925-2009.

Distributed by Itasca Books

The Gendelman Family, 2007: Photograph by Pamela Busby

Cover Design by Sophie Chi
Typeset by Mary Kristin Ross

Printed in the United States of America

Contents

Foreword

1945. An American Jewish GI from Milwaukee confined to a POW slave labor farm in far eastern Germany unexpectedly meets another young soldier, a German Luftwaffe pilot. The American was our father, Max Gendelman. The German, Karl Kirschner, having crash-landed his plane in order to go AWOL from the Nazis, had been hiding out in his grandmother's barn.

From the day they met, Max and Karl formed a lifelong bond.

Family celebrations over the years were punctuated by our father's emotional speeches, which came to be expected and even clamored for. His thoughtful focus on sincere and heartfelt subjects and his word choices often left family and friends alike reaching for tissues. Our father's mother, Grandma Feigel, always added a predictable coda to these speeches—"And Maxie came back from the war"—while she hugged her son, with tears streaming down her face. As children, we mimicked this often-heard phrase in a sing-song chorus, having no idea of the gravity of the events.

Whenever Karl visited Milwaukee, he was treated like a deity. Our four grandparents, each touched by the Nazi murder machine, heaped love, respect, and gratitude on him, as well as tasty Jewish delicacies. For us, the anticipation of Karl's arrival was like waiting for a rock star. It gave our father great pleasure to enjoy his own family's life-cycle events with this very special person. We knew only the outline of their story until recently, when the details unfolded as Max shared the writing of this book.

Our father wrote this story after our urging of many years. It is a true American story: immigrants chasing the American dream, weathering the Depression, and then sending their son back into the cauldron of hate in Europe. He revealed to us not only the horror of combat and prisoner-of-war camps after the Battle of the Bulge, but more important, the rewards of opening one's heart to the possibilities of friendship, with trust and respect, even to an enemy.

In memory of our dear father, we dedicate this book. His enormous strength and suffering made our lives possible. He was the guiding force in our family.

Nina G. Edelman
Lisbeth Amy Rattner
Bruce Paul Gendelman

2013

Prologue

Mortars coughed.
Rockets launched.
88s roared.
Screaming meemies belched their death song.
All the explosions turned night into day.
      —John Toland, *Battle: The Story of the Bulge*

It was a very cold, dark night. I was on the Belgium-German border.
It was 5:30 a.m., December 16, 1944.
The world exploded in front of and all around us.

The ground shook as hundreds of enemy tanks pressed forward, bombarding our positions—Company L, 394th Infantry Regiment, 99th Division. This was the area of the Losheim Gap, where the German army planned to break through our lines, encircle our forces, destroy two armies, and then demand an end to the war.

Hitler's master plan, called the "Watch on the Rhine," had officially begun.

This is the story of how one of the biggest battles of WWII—or of any war that the United States has ever fought—led to an improbable friendship that would last my entire life.

Chapter One

Before

E very story has a beginning and an end.

I know my beginning and can foresee the end.

In between, I have lived a life that has been full of promises, sadness, happiness, adventure, and success.

My main success is in my wonderful, devoted family—one that I am so lucky to have, a family that has been my blessing, my inspiration, my goal.

My family: a beautiful, devoted wife and three lovely and talented children. Each child is married to a wonderful spouse, and their unions have blessed me with ten splendid grandchildren. I am truly a lucky man.

But, to the beginning.

My name is Max Gendelman. I was born in Milwaukee, Wisconsin, on August 15, 1923. I have celebrated that day all my life as my birthday. However, late in my life, when requiring an official birth record, I learned that my birthday was really August 14. Having given birth to me near midnight on the fourteenth, my mother told me that I had been born on the fifteenth. My dear mother, Feigel, which means "a little bird," always felt it was the fifteenth, and my wonderful, devoted mother was always correct—so the fifteenth it remained.

We lived in a Jewish neighborhood in Milwaukee, in an area around Tenth and Walnut Streets. We were a poor family but not destitute. I never had the privilege of ever meeting and knowing my father's parents, my paternal grandparents, but we lived for several years with my maternal grandparents, Lable and Itka Zilberbrand, affectionately known to me as Zaide and Bubbe, who had come to Milwaukee from the Ukraine.

Most immigrants who arrive in this wonderful land of America end up in New York. So what happened? Why Wisconsin? That is a story in itself.

In 1912, Lable left the chaos of Russia. He had lived with his family in a small village in the Ukraine area near Minsk, Ugederrga, but feeling threatened by the Russian regime that had become very anti-Semitic, he decided to leave and get a new start in America. Lable left behind his wife and six children, but he promised to work hard and save money in order to bring them to the free land.

When Lable came to America, he arrived where his cousin, Shalom Roitblatt, was living. Shalom had a small farm in Wisconsin. Lable decided almost instantly that being a farm laborer didn't suit him, and he moved to live with other distant relatives in the city of Milwaukee.

There, he worked as a tailor. The income was not enough for him to live on and save to bring his family over, so he decided to get a carriage and an old horse, which he used for peddling rags and junk or anything he could resell. He lived alone, worked long hours, and after eight years—including the interruption of WWI—he sent enough money for his family to travel to America.

Itka, crippled from birth, was strict but loving. Left in Russia with three boys and three girls, she became the real head of the family. She sewed underwear to support the family until they were able to start their journey to reach Lable in Milwaukee.

My mother, Feigel, was the oldest of the girls. She was born in 1903. Next in line was Bertha, then Zol, Hyman, Eli, and Rachel, the baby, who was ten years younger than Mother.

My father, David Gendelman, born in 1896, was a strong and handsome young man, who, at the early age of twelve, was apprenticed as a sheet metal worker in the little village of Narodichi, Zhitomir District, Ukraine.

He would tell us stories of how he carried hundred-pound bundles of tin up a ladder and onto a roof. He learned the trade well, and it stayed with him the rest of his life.

As a youth, he learned about being Jewish—the benefits as well as the severe problems it brought to him and his family. Dad had one brother and two sisters. Only one sister, Aunt Chaika, lived in America. The White Russians killed the rest of his family.

My father learned the Siddur, the Jewish ritual prayer book, by heart and was very proficient in all his studies. With the war of 1910 going badly, the Russians forced Dad to enter the army, where he had many harrowing experiences. After serving and fighting for the Russian regime, he returned home to start his life over. That was not to be. He was again a *Jew*.

The pogroms soon started. The economy was not good. Russia had many problems, and needing a scapegoat, they blamed the problems on the Jews. Persecutions took their toll on the family. My father's brother and one sister were taken away and killed.

He realized he had to leave the only home he knew—the country he so valiantly fought for and almost died for—because it no longer recognized Jews as decent citizens of the new Russia. Of Jews and dogs, only dogs would be tolerated.

But in the meantime, he had met my mother. He was twenty-four years old. Feigel was seventeen. It didn't take long for them to fall in love. She was the oldest and, I always felt, the most beautiful of the three sisters. She was slender and well-figured, with long, dark hair; a beautiful, clear complexion; and eyes that reflected her lifelong traits, love, affection, and kindness. With the persecutions in full swing and coming closer to their small village, David needed to convince Feigel's mother, Itka, that it was time for the whole family to leave. He would go with them to be with Feigel, to keep her safe, and eventually to marry her when all were together in America with Lable, her father.

But how to get there? Leaving by road was an impossibility.

David soon became the leader of the entire Zilberbrand clan: Itka; Hyman; his new wife, Esther; a small son, Leo; Zoll; Eli; Feigel; Bertha; and little Rachel—with him, a total of ten.

David procured a large rowboat and outfitted it with extra seats. He packed some meager belongings, provisions, food, ropes, and whatever he thought would be needed for the trip.

On the next dark night, they started their perilous journey down the waterways of Russia to what they hoped would be their journey to freedom.

David directed the entire operation. Tasks were assigned; there was much to be done with so many in a small boat. At night they quietly drifted down the river, staying as close to the banks as possible. In most areas, the vegetation at the shoreline helped give them some protection from being discovered. When they did get stuck in shallow water, David would put ropes around his waist and forehead and pull the boat down the river like a horse and wagon. Zoll often helped in the pulling, but Hyman did not because his new wife insisted his place was next to her and her son. That was always a sore subject between the two, then and later in life.

The group finally left Russia and drifted through most of Poland. Eventually they were able to ditch the boat and board a train to the west, to the coast, where they negotiated bookings on a low-priced ship that catered to refugees going to the New World. But before that, while in Warsaw, my father found a rabbi, and a simple wedding took place— David and Feigel together, always.

After more documents were submitted by Lable and more money was sent, Itka and all of her children except Feigel sailed for New York. Lable would meet them at Ellis Island.

Because my father did not have a visa, and Feigel had become his wife, they went to Cuba, a country where the quota was not yet filled. They worked and waited their turn to get a visa to go to America. In Havana, my father used his trade as a tinsmith to make a living. He would pick up scrap metal, mostly tin, and cut and shape it into pots, pans, and bowls. He would give the cookware to my mother, who would sell it in the street and in an open market.

A tinsmith saw my father's work and invited him to work with him in his sheet metal firm, doing roofing, guttering, and covering wood tables with metal (stainless steel) for use in restaurants. The firm became successful. My father was offered a full partnership, but that was not his goal. He dreamed of going to America. He was fully aware that America was a land, not of streets paved with gold but of freedom—the freedom to work, to pray, and to prosper as one wished.

On May 5, 1922, my sister, Esther, was born in Cuba. In the same group of refugee houses was a young widow named Sheindel, who had a four-year-old son named Jack. My parents and Sheindel became close. Soon afterward, however, the Gendelmans received their visas and parted company with their newfound friends, not to find each other again until many years later. It probably was written in the stars that Esther would get married to Jack, whom she met when she was just a few months old.

The Gendelman family of three set sail for America and then traveled to Milwaukee, where once again they would be together with my mother's family.

Lable and Itka made room for the new Cuban arrivals. The meeting was extremely emotional, with hugs, tears, kisses, and thanks to the Almighty.

America became my family's home.

My memory of early childhood is very sketchy. Until the age of five, I spoke only Yiddish. My parents were then taking English lessons at night at the local community hall to prepare them for citizenship.

At age five, I went to early kindergarten at Lloyd Street School. The teacher had a hard time with me, since I knew no English. I did not understand her instructions and just stared and cried with frustration. But with help from another teacher, who spoke Yiddish, I soon was able to understand and to communicate.

In our home, my parents tried their hardest to speak to my sister and me in broken English. They spoke half in English—which they learned at night school—and half in Yiddish, with a bit of Russian thrown in. When they didn't want us to understand what they were saying, they spoke completely in Russian.

I remember having a little dog named Delli. It was a gift from my cousin, Max Feldman. Max was the youngest son of Chaika, my father's sister. At an early age, Max was an entrepreneur. He was handsome, smart, very likable, and extremely devoted to his mother and our family as well. We became close and remained so until his death.

I loved that dog, but for some unknown reason, my mother gave it away. I was heartbroken. I learned a lesson at the tender age of eight; that is, parents aren't always perfect. They, too, can make mistakes. This was the time of the Depression, so I now surmise that feeding another mouth—if only a small dog's—was just too much for them to handle.

The Great Depression started in 1929, just as my father's sheet metal, heating, and roofing business was starting to show great promise. He was doing work for several contractors.

By 1930, many businesses had fallen flat, and the contractors who owed my father money were the first to collapse. His receivables were worthless. In the same year, the banks failed, and the Security Bank on Twelfth Street—the institution that held my father's money—simply closed its doors. At that time, there was nothing like the FDIC to guarantee deposits. The bank president committed suicide. We lost all of our deposited money.

Food was scarce, but we always had something to eat. It was then I learned the importance of even a penny. If I had a penny, I felt rich and was able to go to the corner store and select from an assortment of "penny candies." Even now, more than seven decades later, I will pick up a penny. To me, it can never be worthless.

Once again, my father started to make pots, pans, and garbage can covers for my mother to resell at an open market. And once again, he became a specialist in covering wooden tables with stainless steel. The covering of wood tables with stainless steel was decreed by the city for health reasons. That ruling came at the most opportune time.

It was always our custom to have the "big meal" of the day at noon, for which my father always came home. The main course was served first, with soup and salad being the final course. One of our favorite meals was an old Russian favorite, cabbage borsht with beets and meat. We always had Jewish rye bread. We rubbed the crust of the bread with garlic. To us, that was a hearty meal.

One day I had this meal, with plenty of fresh garlic, and returned to school for the afternoon session. The teacher started sniffing, going from student to student, trying to find where the strong odor was coming from. And then he came to me. I was not only ashamed but also scared. I wanted to go home. Instead, he had me trade places with another student nearer the window. Then he opened the window wide and said, "Max, do us all a great favor. Use the garlic at your evening meal." In his kindness, he taught me a great lesson, and in so doing, he set the standard for me to judge other teachers.

My dad bought an old home on Fifteenth Street near North Avenue. He remodeled it, and the first floor became our living quarters. The second floor, he rented. Later, my mother's younger brother, Eli, married a lovely lady, Ida, and they moved upstairs. This home was set back to the rear of the lot. In front, Dad built a nice duplex to house my grandparents. Later, he built a four-family home on Fourteenth Street and sold it to my grandfather, who lived there for many years. My job was to water the lawn at both buildings and then cut the grass. It seemed that I was always working, but since it was beneficial for the family welfare, I had no objections.

My grandfather gave up peddling when his horse died. It was an old horse, but I missed going with my zaide to feed it in the evening. His wagon gave out at the same time. He bought a small grocery store on Sixth and Vliet Street. This area became a mecca for the Zilberbrands. A drugstore started on another corner, across from the grocery store. The druggist, a young man named Joe Laiken, became well known and well liked. Joe would later marry the youngest Zilberbrand daughter, Rachel. On Fifth and Vliet, the oldest son, Hyman, also started a grocery store, which later moved to Eighth and Walnut Streets.

During the Depression years, I vividly remember my parents taking my sister and me, ages seven and eight, to the local taverns on Friday nights. The taverns all had family entrances where children could be brought in, and for the price of a five-cent beer, we were fed fish, potatoes, and some other wonderful food. Oh, what five cents meant in those days.

As it turned out, my father was clever in real estate. In about 1938, he bought a two-story old home on Nineteenth and Wright and remodeled it into a four-family. We then moved into the upper front and rented out the rest. It was pleasant but small. My sister and I still slept in the same bedroom in twin beds, but the room was so tiny that the door would not close. For many years, we slept with the door open. This became our family residence until after the war and even after I got married.

We were so close to my school that when the first bell rang, my mother would wake me up. I had all of thirty minutes to wash, dress, eat, and get to my classroom before the tardy bell rang.

My brother, Sheldon, was born on October 5, 1930, and quickly became the favorite and the center of the family, with his cute, long, blond curly hair. It was during his young childhood that he became attached to dogs, a love that has stayed with him to this day. Esther and I always enjoyed taking care of him. I remember the little game Sheldon liked to play when we lived on Fifteenth Street. He would find our little dog, Delli, pick it up, and try to toss it down the few steps on the porch. We were always there to make sure the dog never got hurt. Even so, the little dog loved him.

As I approached puberty, my sex education was nil. For some reason, my parents felt there wasn't any hurry to tell me anything. I was ignorant on the subject. My sister, Esther, and I were only fifteen months apart and raised almost like twins. Until the age of six, we bathed together, and we shared the same bedroom. For us, gender was not an issue. Of course, we were aware of our physical differences, but we never thought much of it. I remember when, at about the age of twelve, I was at Larry Duckler's home, and the subject of sex arose. I went along with the discussion, not really caring. When he asked me if I knew how babies were born, I said that I really didn't know. Larry then started to graphically explain the act. I got so angry at his telling me such a terrible lie about my angelic mother that I got up and hit him before walking out in disgust. Later, I apologized.

My high school was North Division High School, where some twenty years earlier, Golda Meir was a student. I was always a good student and popular but never had an active social life. I did become president of both the speech class and chess club. The experiences would prove valuable later. I graduated in three and a half years. When asked, "What was the rush?" the answer was always, "I don't know." I guess the real answer was that I was always on the go, eager to see where the road would take me.

I worked at my father's business, which had survived the Depression and began to grow again. He was doing well in the business of wholesaling the roofing materials he purchased for his own needs. He would sell roofing and nails to builders and other small roofers.

His one truck driver would take out a load each morning and generally return late afternoon. When I drove the truck, I made the deliveries all by myself, unloaded the heavy roofing materials, and placed the items near the house. Then I would return to the shop within an hour or so. Doing the heavy work helped develop my shoulder and bicep muscles. This proved helpful to me in later years, when carrying heavy backpacks, two rifles, and ammunition.

After working the summer, I knew—just as my grandfather had known with farm labor—that roofing would never be my vocation. I enrolled for a semester in February 1941 at the State Teachers College in Milwaukee, now the University of Wisconsin—Milwaukee. But before college started, my friend Norman Eckstein and I took a trip by train to New York City with about a hundred dollars in each of our pockets. This was my first trip alone; my first trip away from the family into an exciting world that dazzled me.

On the long ride from Chicago to New York, we sat across from a mother with two daughters. I became infatuated with one, and during the trip, we managed to be alone to hug and kiss, but I never saw her again.

We were lucky to get a hotel reservation at the famous Astor Hotel, with a room overlooking Times Square. A whole new world was there for our viewing. The trip changed me; my goals were notched a lot higher. I decided to reach for the moon and beyond. Obviously, our money didn't last long. The last few days, we were counting pennies, but at the same time, we were counting our blessings. We made it back home happy but broke. That trip became the "Education of Max Gendelman."

I came back and registered at the University of Wisconsin—Madison for the fall semester. Attending this beautiful university has always been a much-cherished part of my life. Three of my close friends, Larry, Sam and Norman, also went to Madison at the same time. We rented a large, furnished home on Regent Street for fifty-five dollars per month, utilities included. The college entrance fee was then only thirty-nine dollars per semester.

*

On a particularly warm Sunday, we were having a touch football game near our house on Regent Street. Suddenly, we were interrupted by a neighbor shouting, "The Japanese have started a war with America! They bombed Pearl Harbor!" This was December 7, 1941.

This was the end of many of our plans and the beginning of many new ones.

My dear mother often repeated the Yiddish proverb: "Man plans and God laughs."

We hurried back home to listen to the news and await the speech from our president, Franklin Delano Roosevelt. One will always remember his words about the bombing of Pearl Harbor: "Yesterday, December 7, 1941, a date which will live in infamy …"

I was now in my sophomore year at the university and was enrolled in ROTC (Reserve Officers Training Program). I was asked to complete this year and then be a candidate for officer's training (OTC).

That year, I gave up the house and moved into Mrs. Bornstein's, where I shared a room with several other guys. Mrs. Bornstein had three bedrooms on the second floor, two of which she rented; the third was for her two daughters. Hers was a kosher home, and five nights per week she prepared a kosher evening meal, included in our rental, that she also served to about six other students. Being a widow, this is how she made her living.

One night, shortly after moving into our room, I heard someone crying in the next room. I entered to see a sixteen-year-old student in tears. I introduced myself and inquired as to the problem. I soon found out. His name was Phil Schneider, and it was his first time away from home. He was lonely and scared. I introduced him to my other room-mates and said, "Phil, we are now going to have a beer and pizza."

"But I've never had a beer or pizza," said Phil. I responded, "You will now!"

From that moment, Phil and I were inseparable. His father would send Phil his monthly allowance, plus some extra, and would jokingly insist that I audit and certify his expenditures. Phil and I remained close friends through the years.

At least once or twice a month on Sundays, my mother, father, brother, and sometimes my sister would drive the eighty miles to have a picnic with mother's *"Shaine, Libbe, Zisse, Zin Meine"* (pretty, lovely boy of mine). She would bring enough food for the entire group. Gasoline was strictly rationed, so my mother's family would help with the gas for the trips to Madison.

Once a week I sent home my laundry in a special case on the Milwaukee to Madison commuter bus called the Badger bus. Dad would pick it up at the station, and after my laundry was washed, he would send it back. Many students followed this practice. Even with the bus fare, it was cheaper than having it done by a laundry service. And when my laundry was returned, there were always delicious goodies that kept me happy.

Life seemed very simple on the surface but was troublesome underneath.

With the world being torn apart by Hitler and Mussolini and his Arab friends, I became very restless. I had good grades and could have applied for a transfer to medical school, as there was a great need for doctors. This would have given me an exemption from the draft, but I never seriously considered that an option. I did not want to be an officer and go to OTC. I probably would have been called late in 1943. Instead, I decided to enlist and maybe get stationed close to home for my basic training.

After spending the next few weeks finishing the semester, straightening out some affairs, and bidding farewell to my friends and teachers—which was not easy, as I loved living in Madison and was happy to be attending the university—I moved back to Milwaukee and to my beloved family. Knowing that I would be leaving soon created a tension that was very apparent. My mother kept crying, hugging, and kissing me; she would look at me from afar. Memories had to be constantly renewed and updated.

Never known as a Don Juan, I really never had a steady girlfriend. The closest was Shirley Taxen, the daughter of my barber. When we finally said our good-byes, I promised to write and hoped to come back after the war to take up where we left off.

But the other good-byes were heartbreaking. I thought that my mother would faint several times. She kept a wet *schmatte* on her chest, trying to console herself. My strong-willed father, tough as nails when he had to be, couldn't stop crying.

The electric train from Milwaukee to Fort Sheridan, Illinois, was ready to leave. We all embraced and cried some more. I took aside my twelve-year-old brother, Shel, and told him it was my hope that he would not have to fight in a war. This was to be the war to end all wars.

The train left, carrying me to a new, exciting, difficult life. My life was about to change forever.

Chapter Two

Private Max Gendelman

February 25, 1943, was the day that I became Private Max NMI Gendelman, 36807750. I never had a middle name, but now I had one. NMI really stood for "no middle initial," but my sergeant kept referring to me as "not (having) much intelligence." It was up to me to prove him wrong.

The serial number is embedded in one's memory. No GI ever forgets his number; he becomes a number and, hopefully, will not die too soon with this number.

After a short indoctrination, we filled out a variety of forms—insurance, next of kin, an intelligence test, etc. I was then told I would be part of a group that was to be sent to Fort Lewis, Washington. This was as far away from Milwaukee as they could possibly have sent me and still be in the States.

We were put on a coach troop train—no sleepers, no sleeping facilities, and very few facilities of any kind.

This torturous journey took eight days and nights before we reached our destination. There were few double sets of rail tracks going from east to west. Regularly scheduled trains had priority on the use of the rails. Quite often, we were sidelined for many hours, waiting for a train to pass. Whenever we approached a populated area, and also at night, we had to pull the shades down for security reasons, as the movement of troops was secret.

After the second day, I could not sleep on the hard bench chair. I claimed a section of the overhead luggage rack—a wire rack—and slept there. Others saw what I did, and soon all the racks were used for sleeping

Finally, we arrived at our home on the Pacific, Fort Lewis, south of Seattle. Once again we went through indoctrination and were given another, more extensive IQ test.

I was in the infantry. I was to train to become a good soldier. Therefore, to become a well-trained soldier, we were awakened at 6 a.m. every day and had only thirty minutes to do the three "S's" (shit, shave, and shower). At 6:30 we had to assemble at the company parade grounds with our assigned squad. In the middle of winter, on the Pacific Coast at 6:30 in the morning, the sun is still not up. It was pitch-black outside and unbelievably cold! Roll call was taken and uniforms inspected. Then we exercised. Finally, we were dismissed and ran to the chow barracks for a hot, welcome breakfast.

Mind you, as a young Jewish man growing up in a kosher home, I never ate pork, bacon, or ham. Now that I was in the army, I certainly had no choice but to eat this food. I learned to eat it, and I especially loved the crispy bacon.

I realized that so far, my education had been negligent as it related to sex and bacon. I tried bacon; I liked it. So maybe sex would be my next experience to try and like.

We were getting our basic training, in preparation for the big time, seeing action in either of the fronts, Europe or the Pacific. We all had to learn fast, for we were told, "Your life and the lives of your fellow soldiers depend on how well you learn the basics of being a disciplined soldier."

Shortly after arriving, we were given M-1 rifles and taught to use, disassemble, clean, and reassemble them—while blindfolded. We learned to live with our rifle. The M-1 was to become our very best friend, who, when called upon, would save our lives.

We received shooting instructions and were on a course, shooting at targets about 150 yards away. Until then, I had never shot a rifle in my life. In ROTC we had wooden guns that we used in training. Jewish boys were seldom exposed to guns in their homes and neighborhoods.

I have a problem with closing or winking my left eye. When shooting, one closes the left eye and sees the target with the right. In order to do that,

I found I had to gently tap the eye, close the eyelid, concentrate on the target, and then shoot. As I was finishing my turn shooting at the target and while still on the ground, a lieutenant came up to me. I quickly got up, saluting as required. He looked at my name tag and said, "Gendelman, where did you learn to shoot like that?" I was not sure what to say. Did I do so terribly bad? Surprised, I didn't immediately answer. "Gendelman, you are an excellent marksman—so far, the very best of the entire group." That day's results awarded me the Marksman Medal, a medal that later changed the course of my life in the army and afterwards. Not bad for a Jewish boy. Maybe it was the crisp bacon. Who could tell?

After several weeks of basic, I was called to general headquarters and told that the general's assistant, a lieutenant colonel, wanted to talk to me. I wondered how and when I'd screwed up.

In the meeting, I was informed my IQ test results were in, and I had the highest grade of the new recruits. The test showed I had a superior grade in most categories. He gave me an offer that I could not refuse. I was asked to join the intelligence division. Without hesitation, I agreed.

The next few weeks were very interesting. I continued my basic training but had special courses in intelligence operations. One time I flew with the general in a Cub plane and surveyed the bivouac areas during a field maneuver. This was a special exercise for all troops on setting up emergency living facilities on the frontline.

On or about May 7, 1943, the colonel called me into his office. He had previously offered to recommend me for Officers Training Core (OTC), but I had refused. I didn't want to be an officer and make the army my life's work. And I felt I could not give anyone orders to go on a mission that would send him to a certain death.

Now, he said, "Max, I highly recommend you accept a transfer to ASTP [Army Specialized Training Program] to learn engineering. You will be assigned immediately. Time is of the essence, for in the next few days our entire division in training will be sent overseas to Europe."

I readily accepted, thanked him, and wished him luck and a safe return to America and to his loved ones. I left to pack my bags and to go to my next assignment. I was to be trained as an engineer at Brookings State College in Brookings, South Dakota.

The story was that Brookings was built where two cow paths crossed, but that was not really so. Brookings was a small town with a small college. We were warmly greeted and quickly felt at home in our new environment.

Being a lot closer to Milwaukee, Mom, Dad, Esther, and Shel were able to drive up several months later. We spent a few days together, sharing the news, mixed with laughter and tears of joy. "Parting is such sweet sorrow" is so true; it took a great toll on my mother. We said our good-byes once again, not knowing when we would next see one another.

Social life in Brookings was quite limited, although it did have a bowling alley, a good local restaurant, and a theater. On Saturday nights, there was always a dance at a local bar club.

South Dakota was a "dry" state. When attending the dance, we would bring our own liquor and buy the setup—a bottle of club soda for five dollars. Money was scarce, so I would buy the cheapest alcohol that I could—rum. I'd never really drunk liquor before, and the first time I attended this dance, I got high. I met a young lady who seemed to enjoy being with soldiers. As the evening wore on and drinks were consumed, I took a walk with her. I don't really remember much after that, and I'm not sure if I made a fool of myself; I only remember waking up back in my room. That was the last time I drank rum or any other liquor at Brookings.

Our engineering studies were cut short, six months before we were to get our degree from the ASTP course. The entire program had been discontinued and all participants reassigned to continue with basic training before being sent overseas. I was sent to Fort Leonard Wood, Missouri, about eighty miles south of St. Louis. The training was intense. The weather was stinking hot, and the ticks were a painful problem for me. We had to crawl on the ground in the fields, under actual live machine gun fire. The ticks imbedded themselves into my skin, and the only way to get them out was to light a cigarette and place the burning end to the spot where the tick entered. They, too, couldn't stand the heat and would finally come out.

We all looked forward to some time off on weekends when training was not scheduled.

One weekend, I was given a three-day pass for R&R (rest and recuperation). In the evenings, there was little if any transportation to St. Louis. I left on a Thursday evening and hitched a ride to St. Louis. I was picked up, and the driver said he would take me all the way to where I wanted to go. However, he had to make a few quick stops along the highway. On the front seat next to me was a white satin pillow and on it sat a .38 handgun. He saw my doubts but reassured me he only used the gun for protection. Several times, he signaled certain oncoming trucks with his searchlight, and they would pull over. He would have a brief conversation with the driver and then we'd continue on.

I never found out what that was all about, but it was great to get to the city. I rented a room, got into a hot bathtub, and soaked for what seemed like hours. Most guys would be out "catting," but I was happy to get some rest, a good meal, and a beer. I cherished the time to be by myself. I had time to think about where my life was headed. I had no control over that decision, but I knew that I would be well prepared mentally as well as physically for the journey ahead.

Shortly afterward, we were given our orders, and I was on the move again. This time I was going to England for the opportunity to face the German juggernaut.

We were transferred to a debarkation camp near New York and given some time off, as well as permission to meet with our loved ones before our Liberty ship would take us to England. We were warned not to tell our families or close friends where we were going or when or how. I called home and told my parents that if they came to New York soon, I would be able to see them for a short while. They did come, and we spent several afternoons together. Finally, I told them it was time to leave. Once again, parting was such heartbreak for my parents as well as for me. When the final moment came to say good-bye, my dear, tough father, with tears streaming down his face, related the story of when he was a soldier. There were many times he thought his end was near. He would pray to his God. He would say the S'hma, the affirmation of belief in his love for God.

*Hear, O Israel: the Lord is our God, the Lord is one. You
shall love the Lord your God with all your heart, with
all your soul, with all your might ... (Deuteronomy 6:4)*

I promised my father I would certainly remember my family and my God. My mother made me promise I would come back home, safe and sound. She needed me, her *shaine zisse kind*. She suffered so.

After they left, I felt so sad, so lonely, so heartbroken, wondering and thinking if I would ever see my family again. Only God knew.

Finally, we boarded our Liberty ship for a voyage that took about thirty days to cross the Atlantic. The mass-produced ship had poor facilities for use as a troop carrier. It was used mainly to bring war goods and supplies to England. Many were sunk by German U-boats, but enough of them got through that it was worth the risk. Supplies were needed.

We were in a large convoy of many different ships, escorted on the perimeter by several destroyers. The ships were strung out for miles, and it became apparent that protecting all the ships was impossible. Several were sunk. We were lucky.

January on the Atlantic is no fun. Our little ship was tossed violently by the storms and huge waves. Meals were generally "tossed" too, whenever we had bad weather conditions. The hold where we slept was miserably hot, stuffy, and foul smelling. We did not have beds. Instead, we slept in rope hammocks, three high. I was lucky and got the highest one. What luck! Ever try climbing into a hammock eight feet above the ground?

All good things must come to an end. We made it to the White Cliffs of Dover.

And when we finally disembarked, I thanked the Almighty for seeing us through and getting us off that stinking ship.

England, we are here!

Chapter Three

An Innocent Abroad

Being in England and being able to see London was a dream come true. The farthest I had ever been from home before enlisting was New York City, when my friend Norman and I visited for a week after we graduated from high school.

We were assigned to a British Air Force base to have further training and field exercises while awaiting final orders. The invasion of Europe by crossing the channel and landing in France was our guess. Nobody but the highest echelon really knew. General Dwight D. Eisenhower was in complete charge of all the armies. He wanted to keep the place and time a total secret but would purposely "leak" false information to keep the enemy guessing.

On weekends, we were free to visit London. I was amazed at the extreme destruction this city had suffered. V-2 rockets and the German Luftwaffe had taken their toll, but there were still some areas where the damage was limited and life continued. Some pubs and restaurants were open. Good food was scarce, but fish and chips were still plentiful, and when downed by British ale, it tasted just fine. Compared to the food on the trip over, the fish was heavenly. In the weeks ahead, I had my share of this British delicacy.

Meanwhile, I had some family business to take care of. My cousin Sam Feldman had been overseas and had met a girl in London. Her name was Rita. Sam's brother, Max, asked me to "check her out" and see what she was like. Specifically, he wanted me to determine her real intentions.

Did she want to marry Sam in order to come to America or did she really love Sam for himself?

I contacted Rita, met with her family, and spent two evenings trying to get her true feelings for Sam. I was impressed with her. She was a nice, energetic, vivacious, and fast-talking young lady. After the first night, she asked if I would "knock [her] up sometime." I soon learned she meant for me to call her again. She offered to fix me up with some of her girlfriends, but I declined. Socializing was not on my schedule at that time. I gave my blessing to the family and that sealed the deal. Sam and Rita got engaged and later married in America.

London was a city for the *living*. I took advantage of every moment to enjoy each day. I marveled at the history that was evident everywhere. The people were very kind to the American soldiers and slowly grew accustomed to the "night fighters," our black soldiers. The British soldiers were friendly to a point. There was noticeable resentment toward Americans who were catching the eyes of British girls.

Traveling from the base to London we passed typical British communities, where many streets were lined on both sides with hedges built of stones. Later on, these hedges became an important symbol to me.

D-Day was getting closer. Preparations were at a frenzied pace. Everyone was on edge, waiting to be assigned to an active fighting group. We all felt we had enough training and were ready to get the fight started, to defeat the Krauts, and then go back home.

One morning during our daily training, I was approached by an officer and taken aside. I wondered now what I had I done. He introduced himself, ordered me at ease, and said my name had been given to him as being a good candidate for further training as a sniper. The training course was six weeks long and given there in England. Since I had a Marksman Medal for being an expert in marksmanship, I was considered a good candidate.

I asked, "Even if our unit is called for D-Day, does that mean I would still finish the course?"

"Absolutely," he said. "We have a great need for snipers."

I thought this would allow me to miss D-Day and, who knows, maybe the war would be over by then. With that in mind, and with the prospect of enjoying some extra time in London, I said, "Sir, count me in. I'll be glad to be trained as a sniper."

Weekends were a welcome respite from the harsh training. We were given a pass and allowed to go to London. One of the fellow snipers in training was a friendly, tall drink of water, Elliot W. Wager, from Denver, Colorado. We were able to spend some time together in London, sharing stories while downing some warm British ale and nibbling on chips. Time off was always welcomed, and the USO facilities were much appreciated.

A thousand or more ships were on the high seas, flying huge balloons that were held by steel cables. They were used to keep the German air force from flying too low to strafe the ships and debarking soldiers. June 6, 1944—D-Day had begun.

Thousands of men were loaded into landing crafts and driven as close to the shore as possible. They were always under extreme enemy fire from the ground and the air, and they were being blown to bits by hidden bombs in the shallow water.

The landings were mainly in two locations in Normandy, France: Utah Beach and Omaha Beach. Both landings experienced great casualties, but Omaha had the most. Some landing crafts did not get close enough to discharge their men, and when they left the craft, the water was too deep and hundreds drowned while attempting to reach the beach. Those that did reach land were soon killed by the tremendous onslaught of gunfire.

It seemed almost impossible that anyone could have survived, but they did. Small groups held their ground with the assistance of the US weaponry in the form of tanks, trucks, and air force warships.

The casualty losses affected all of us at the school for snipers. Sniper losses were extremely heavy. My training intensified, and the day when I would be sent across the channel was rapidly approaching. The entire group with which I had come to England was already in France. I had only to await my turn.

On or about October 30, 1944, my unit landed in France. The trip across the channel was rough but bearable. Our landing northwest of Paris on the French coast was devoid of gunfire—not like it had been for the troops during the D-Day invasion. The Germans were pushed back about twenty miles from Paris, which was now a free city once again.

We were assembled into a fighting group that shortly saw action. The Germans were still very active, and we had some casualties the very next day. My job was quite simple: Take positions where you can see the enemy. If they are there, or if they are coming toward your area, shoot to kill.

One afternoon I was in a squad of about eight men. We came upon a farmhouse and saw some chickens running around the yard. One of the GIs called me over and said,

"Max, you are Jewish. You Jews always have chicken soup. How about making us some? We got ourselves a nice chicken. Get to work."

I had never made chicken soup before. My mother always made it, and I loved it, but I never bothered to learn how to prepare it myself. How difficult could it be? "Okay," I said. "I'll give it a try."

Some guys built a small fire. I removed the lining from my steel helmet and then filled it with water, hoping it would get hot. Now what do I do with the chicken? I vividly recalled when my mother would take me to the *Shochet,* the kosher butcher. The head was cut off and the chicken hung upside down on a peg so that all the blood would run out. Then he gave the chicken to my mother, who would take the feathers off as best she could. Next, he passed the chicken over an open flame, cleaning off the remaining feathers and searing it. Done!

I admitted to not being a *Shochet* nor would I ever be or want to be.

I took the chicken, held it by the neck and head, and with full force swung the chicken around. A few moments later, I had the head in my hand and the body of the chicken was about ten feet away. I recovered it, cut it as best as I could, and put it all in the helmet—feathers, guts, and all. The water never got very hot, and I was told to test the soup. We couldn't stay around there much longer, afraid of enemy in the area. Reluctantly, I put my cup in the helmet, took out some of the "soup," and took a swig. Only one taste, and I rushed to the nearby bushes and threw up. I heaved and heaved until there was nothing left inside me. The other guys were lucky and smart. They never tasted my concoction.

The fire was killed, my helmet recovered, the contents thrown away, and my lining restored. I was fully aware that I did not possess the cooking talents of my Jewish mother.

Back to the war, even though we were not filled with such a delight—chicken soup.

We fought our way to the coast of Belgium and were joined by thousands of new replacement troops and hundreds of vehicles. Commotion was everywhere!

Belgium was a beautiful country that took a beating but still stood tall in every respect. As we entered the main square in Brussels, I saw the famous fountain with the young boy holding his little penis and water coming out.

Our group was again split up. We all became replacements and were assigned to an active fighting division. I was assigned to the Checkerboard Division, the 99th Infantry, Company L, 394th Regiment, part of the 1st Army. The commanding general was Major General Walter E. Lauer.

The 99th were extremely shorthanded, having suffered many casualties. Company L was short a sniper, so I was very welcome in my new company and fit in well. Their other sniper didn't last too long. I didn't try to become very close to any of the men in my new company. It hurt too much to get too close, knowing that many of them would not be around for very long. You can beat your chest in sorrow, but that is no aid to the living or to the "friend" you just met and lost.

Our company, Company L, was moved up to the front lines in the Hürtgen Forest, part of an eighty-five–mile front facing the border of Germany near Losheim. The Belgium border was separated from the German front by a small river or creek. It was heavily fortified in an area that was the original Siegfried line. This area was lined with concrete "pillboxes," where German soldiers could be quite safe and shoot at our positions with ease. The area was also heavily fortified with land mines designed to kill when activated, and they did kill so many of our men.

The Hürtgen Forest is a very beautiful and picturesque area, but to us, it was a hellhole. We now went to work, creating our new deluxe home. It was winter—November—and this winter was exceptionally cold, coupled with lots of snow. The ground was frozen but digging was a must. Digging we did, piling the dirt around the foxhole, so the German spies could not readily see our places of residence. A problem soon became apparent on days when temperatures rose—the ground would thaw, and we would find ourselves living in miniature pools. The next day it would all freeze, and the cycle would start over again. This was our home, our position, for about six weeks.

The snow, ice, and cold combined to have a demoralizing effect on all of us. It was, however, something we had to live with.

We had no galoshes. We had no suitable winter clothing, few (if any) changes of underwear, and no chance to properly shower. In other words, the situation (and we) stunk. We had to dig a trench deep in the woods for our bathroom and toilet with deluxe plumbing facilities—snow. Imagine trying to squat and relieve yourself with snow several feet deep. The problem was doing all that and still trying to keep hidden from the Germans. We were always worried about getting shot in the ass and trying to explain that to the army nurses, if we were so lucky.

Eating was another problem. When the cooks were able to come up to our area, we generally got one or two hot meals a day. Often, they didn't make it, and we had our "C- rations" (shit in a can, we called it). We always managed to get by.

It was hard to understand why the troops on the front lines, fighting the war, had less than did the military in the cities and rear echelon. We could see soldiers with warm winter parkas, gloves, overcoats, and galoshes, while we had none. That was a question to which I never received a logical answer. I guess maybe they thought we would be killed soon; therefore, we wouldn't have to have the necessities required for good soldiering.

We faced the German Siegfried lines approximately eleven miles south of the city of Höfen. Combat came early for our company. A German machine gun killed our lieutenant, Charles M. Allen. He had headed the patrol that was sent out on a foolish mission to probe the Germans. What good was it to lose good men to say in a report that we saw the enemy and they killed our men? We knew where they were; we knew we were correct.

When a patrol was ordered out "by the powers in the high echelon," whoever they may have been, we knew that many of the men would not come back. The patrol had to cross the river and be in an open field in order to get to the woods where the Germans were hidden in their concrete pillboxes. They waited for our soldiers to foolishly walk into the open, and then they cut them down with machine gun and rifle fire.

Being a sniper, I was not chosen for these patrols. I had other duties and went out by myself, thus giving me a better chance to seek cover and fulfill my designated missions.

I was relatively new and sociable, but I seldom got into discussions with others, as the subject was always the same: booze and women. I generally tried to keep to myself and read during free time. Often, I would grab a pen and a notebook and jot down notes, to remember what was occurring, dates, and thoughts. What I hadn't realized at that point, early on, was how hard it would be to forget.

Mail call was always eagerly awaited. When the mail arrived, once a week if lucky, the clerk would shout out our names and throw the letter to us, as we stood around him with eager expectation. It seemed the name "Gendelman" was generally called out the most often. That, too, created some jealousy and a little problem with the others in my company. Soon that would pass—until the next week when mail would arrive again. Some people wrote to me very often. My mother wrote almost every day. When I read her heartbreaking letters, I always felt like crying from the joy of having such a devoted family. Rabbi Jacob Twerski wrote often as well. I'm sorry I wasn't able to save some of that mail—it would be precious. He was not only our rabbi but also a close friend of my family. He had come from the same area in Russia as my parents. I wrote back as often as I could. The mail was always censored and many times, for some illogical reason, parts of it—even sentences about the weather, whether the sun was shining or not—were crossed out before being forwarded to the person designated. I knew what I could say and could not say, and I always felt I kept within the allowable limits of news to the people to whom I wrote.

Other than the crazy ordered patrols, we saw very little action. Both sides were testing and evaluating. One day, I was called to our captain's tent. Once again, I thought I had screwed up. Captain Allen J. Ferguson asked me to be at ease and to please sit down. He started a conversation that I shall never forget.

"PFC Gendelman, may I call you Max?"

"Yes, sir, please do."

"Good. You see, in my estimation, you are a very different type of soldier. You remind me of how I was when I first joined the service. You learn fast, do your job, and keep your own counsel. Bullshitting with the guys is not your idea of time well spent.

"I have a favor to ask of you. You know that our lieutenant was killed. Battalion headquarters, in all their wisdom, has just instructed me to send out another patrol to further test the German preparedness on our front. I feel that I can't send my sergeant out there alone. I must go and lead the patrol. However, I have a deep feeling that I may never come back. I have here a small package of some of my belongings: a letter to my wife and children, my wedding band, and officer's graduation ring. Please see to it that they get sent back to the rear echelon and to my wife."

I didn't know what to say. "Captain, please take me with you. Maybe I can be of help if pinned down."

"Max, very kind to offer, but you are the only sniper this company has left. No, but thanks for offering."

"Captain, you can be assured I will guard this package with my life and will forward it, if and when required. But please, do me a great favor; come back from the patrol and take care of the package yourself."

Choked up, he said, "If I return, I'd like to be closer friends with you."

"Captain, that would be my greatest wish and truly an honor."

I promised to fulfill his wish. I picked up the package, saluted him, saying, "*My captain, my friend*," and left. Captain Ferguson and his patrol headed out, but I did not see them leave.

The captain never returned. He was killed by machine gun fire from a position that we all knew so well and for a patrol that was pointless.

I wish I had known him better. How useless is the life of an individual soldier in the overall plan. "Man plans, and God laughs." I cried, remembering my mother's words.

Our company was scheduled to be relieved for several welcome days of R&R. We longed for fresh underwear, warm clothes, better boots, and hot food. We were so tired of C-rations and D-bars, a sickening delicacy of concentrated chocolate that gave you the runs. This food was called "Hitler's Secret Weapon." If the Germans didn't kill you, the D-bar would.

For our R&R, we were to go to the little village of Honsfeld, Belgium, which was five miles from the front lines that we had been facing for about six weeks. A rumor spread that Marlene Dietrich was to visit the group, accompanied by the great Glenn Miller. The info on Glenn Miller was correct; not with Marlene, however.

We never got to see Glenn Miller. He was flying into our area when his plane disappeared. To this day, his body has never been found. It is presumed that he ditched into the Channel. What a waste. He was such a fine man and a magnificent musician.

Our luck also was about to run out. The date was December 15, 1944. The 75,000 American troops made little note of this date. The only thing that mattered to our troops was that they were one day closer to a Christmas far from home.

We were along the Ardennes Front—called the "Ghost Front," named after German patrols coming toward us like ghosts in long, white garments—from Echternach to Monschau.

We, the 99th Division, were anchored near Monschau, a historic German border town, which was built in a valley between wooded mountains. Nowhere along the Ghost Front was the feeling of comfortable confidence stronger than at our end, with its northern terminus some eighty-five miles from Echternach. Rumor was that Hitler had bicycled through the cobbled streets and stopped to admire its rococo buildings. He himself then ordered the whole town be treated as a museum and spared the ravages of war. No shells ever landed on Monschau.

Toward the northern end of the 99th, the German's 2nd Division had just moved up from the Schnee Eifel salient—a protruding land formation in the Eifel mountainous region—and was attacking through the 99th lines in a narrow two-mile corridor. They were trying to smash a hole in the Siegfried line, then break through and knife their way to the Roer Dams. These dams, a menace to the entire Allied advance into the Roer Valley, had to be captured before the main attack started. If their sluices were opened, the advancing army could be flooded and cut off from the rear.

At midnight, the men of the 2nd Division were stalled in front of Wahlerscheid, a heavily fortified crossroads.

They waited and watched.

We also were on the alert for patrols, for snipers.

The V-2 rockets the Germans fired on London, which created such damage and havoc, were launched from a wooded area just in front of our lines. You could hear them start out, slowly at first as they climbed toward the sky with their load of destruction; then gathering speed as they rose higher. At the point where they emerged from the tree lines and were still fairly slow, we tried shooting them down. It was a hard job, but we were lucky and able to destroy several rockets. I believe I was successful in hitting and destroying one with my rifle fire. The rocket plunged back toward the earth, near the front, and cheers went up.

We also waited and watched.

At the same time, the plan to change the course of history through mass destruction had begun. Hitler personally created and put into action his master plan, "Operation Watch on the Rhine."

GERMANY'S LAST STAND—A Very Brief History

"Operation Watch on the Rhine" was Hitler's name for his new and final military plan for victory.

He remembered the history of Frederick the Great, whose greatest battle, against all odds, became Germany's greatest victory. On December 7, 1944, Hitler called together his entire general staff and gave them his battle plans for one daring drive that would win the war for Germany.

"Christrose" was the plan's code name. It was the most brilliant and most deceptive attack ever launched on the Western Front. The plan would soon start.

Hitler's general staff consisted of:
Field Marshal Wilhelm Keitel, supreme commander of all the armies
General Alfred Jodl, chief of operations
General Heinz Guderin, tank commander
General Kriefe, personal representative of Field Marshal Goering
General Rudolf Gercke, chief of transportation

General Jodl, who drew up much of the plan, presented it to the staff. At first, most generals were reluctant to put this daring plan into operation. If not successful, they knew the war would be over. But the great Hitler, would not be deterred. Wasn't he the greatest general? Of course, he must be!

Lt. Col. Friedrich August Freiherr (Baron) von der Heydte was Germany's famous paratroop commander. As a student, he had received a scholarship from the Carnegie Endowment for International Peace in 1933. In spite of his intellectual doubts as to the merits of the Watch on the Rhine, he was excited at the prospect of his troops playing a part in fulfilling Hitler's plan. However, when he heard that Josef Dietrich, "Sepp," would be his army commander, he had second thoughts. He was appalled. He felt Dietrich was way over his head as commander of a division. Hitler had given Dietrich this honor, this award, for being "the Butcher of Bavaria."

General Kriefe reported the Luftwaffe had 350 planes, including eighty new jets at the ready and more available, when needed, after the foul weather broke.

To cross the Rhine River, bridges were reinforced and tracks laid. Ferries were modified in case the bridges were destroyed. Five Panzer—German tank armor—divisions were to be withdrawn from the Eastern Front against Russia. A total of twelve Panzer divisions and eighteen to twenty infantry divisions (the entire 7th Army) was the initial force designated to start the blitz of the west. The plan was simple. They would cross the River Meuse between Liege and Namur, bypass Brussels and reach Antwerp, Belgium, on the coast within seven days, breaking through at Losheim and confronting our company head on. This became known as the Losheim Gap or "the Bulge."

Unfortunately for Private Max Gendelman, that was immediately in front of Company L, the 99th Division—my position.

The Germans planned to smash the western Allied armies. Thirty American and British divisions would be cut in half, annihilated, and forced to sue for a separate peace.

Two hundred fifty thousand men and thousands of tanks, artillery, and vehicles of all kinds were made ready for the great battle. Trails and roads were matted with straw to help keep the noise down as the Germans advanced to the front to take up their positions in preparation for the "Great Day."

Three German armies were moved more than ten miles through the woods to their new final position. Infantry divisions were moved to a line about six miles from the front, accompanied by horse-drawn guns and howitzers. Many of the cannons and howitzers were from World War I.

Positions were taken in the Hürtgen Forest, across from the Meuse River and across from our area, Losheim.

Just before midnight on December 15, 1944, the German soldiers in the offensive gathered around their assault posts, standing in the bitterly cold night to listen to a message that officers read from Field Marshal Gerd von Rundstedt: *"Soldiers of the Western Front! Your great hour has arrived. Large attacking armies have started against the Anglo-Americans. I do not have to tell you more than that. You feel it yourself. We gamble everything! You carry with you the holy obligation to give everything to achieve things beyond human possibilities for our Fatherland and our Führer."* Deutschland über alles!

Hours later, 5:30 a.m., Hitler's Operation Christrose began.

For the Americans, this would be called the Battle of the Bulge, one of the greatest battle ever fought in World War II or in any other American war.

German armies pushed ahead in our area and on the eighty-five–mile Ghost Front. Their main focus was at Losheim, where they successfully broke through, creating what became known as the Losheim Gap.

The three attacking armies consisted of the 6th Panzer on the north, the 5th in the center, and the 7th Panzer in the south.

We were the first to be hit. All control between us—the 14th Cavalry group—and our higher echelon was broken. This was the northern end of the Hürtgen Forest called the Ardennes Forest. Our front attacked by more than fifty German columns.

The main attack against us was by the 12th SS Panzer Division and the 276th Volksgrenadier Division of the 6th Panzer Army. They smashed through the positions of the 99th, toward fulfilling their goal of crossing the Meuse River between Liege and Namur, and pushed west toward the coast—to Antwerp. Hitler's plan, his dream, was well underway.

This was Hitler's weather: fog, drizzle, haze, low clouds. The foul weather kept our airplanes from attacking and coming to our assistance. No one came to our assistance.

At 6:30 a.m., the shelling stopped. The German infantry advanced, coming out of the fog and the mist. Our communication with headquarters was disrupted by shelling. The radios were jammed. We had no officers left to lead and direct.

With the enemy coming, I had to move fast. I grabbed two rifles: my sniper rifle (a 1903 Springfield with telescope sights) and my M-1. I also grabbed some ammunition, C-rations, backpack, and shovel. Then I quickly bade farewell to my wet, miserable home of six weeks. Personal items, such as photos, letters, and the package from Captain Ferguson, had to be left behind. I hoped our troops would later find it and get it to his wife. The package had her name and address on it.

My duties as a sniper had me often going out alone, thinking for myself in order to fulfill my mission and at the same time stay alive. Once again, my training kicked in. The attack was coming from both sides. I decided to go straight—straight to and through the middle of the approaching juggernaut.

I could not determine the status of our regiment or division but assumed they had been decimated by the furious attack, by the huge number of men and amount of equipment that had been thrown at them.

For all practical purposes, Co. L had been wiped out—no longer a fighting force. Ninety-nine percent of the 2nd Platoon of Co. L were casualties. Most had been killed or taken prisoner. Only one man of the original forty managed to get back to the 99th Division at Elsenborn. He was PFC Charles Swann. When he reported to the Co. L commanding officer and asked the whereabouts of the 2nd Platoon, the CO replied, "You're it."

Only twenty-eight men of the 185 in Co. L survived.

Hundreds of other GIs wandered around, just going but not sure where. Soldiers were lying dead in the open fields. The dead were by the hundreds—Germans as well as Americans. Nothing could help them. If they had extra ammo, I relieved them of that but could do nothing else.

I used up most of my ammo, shooting at approaching troops. Hundreds of isolated clashes were going on all around me. Hit and run. I often wondered if the German men I killed had wives, children, and loving families. But thoughts like that, if dwelled upon too long, would just get you killed. The Germans, too, were shooting at you. You had to shoot back but be more accurate and deadlier.

Most of that first day, December 16, became a blur. Shooting, running, hiding, advancing, and fighting, and then escaping again to shoot and run and hide.

I again stayed to myself, not wishing to form any alliances, this time because I didn't want to have to explain any of my actions. I had to be free to take off and keep my destiny in my own hands. It seems this became my pattern for the rest of my life.

The first night I spent deep in the woods. I found a large tree that had fallen and worked myself under the tree, creating my "foxhole." I covered myself with the snow-covered leaves and ground and tried to sleep. I was able to doze off and sleep intermittently, with my rifle cradled in my arm. Again, the weather was bitterly cold. The ground was wet and icy. My feet were always damp, and it was at this time they became frozen. I was cold, hungry, and feeling alone in this godforsaken part of the world—Germany.

When I did sleep, I continued to have dreams of my family. My mother was looking at me, with her loving plea to take me in her arms. I told her I'd be home soon. Tears came down my father's unshaven face. He was worried I might never come home again. My dear sister and brother were there too. Oh, how I missed them.

I had to constantly rub my feet and hands to keep the circulation going. Dawn was breaking and with that, I gave official notice to my landlord that I was vacating the room that had been my home for the night. I cleaned off some fresh snow, ate some for water, and started to travel deeper into German territory, the land the SS Panzer troops controlled.

The shelling had begun anew. The weather was still overcast, but it got warmer, bringing a mist of rain, snow, and sleet and the sounds of enemy in the area. I treated myself to one of the few rations left and, once again faced the turmoil and chaos of war.

The plan was the same—walk, hide, and give thanks I was still alive.

GIs were everywhere. Some were alive and walking in circles. Others were dead, their travels prematurely ended. If the dead had rations, I appropriated them. Most had no ammo or rifles. They were discarded when the ammo ran out.

That afternoon, while walking, I was approached by a sergeant of the 394th. He asked if he could travel with me. He felt we could help each other. He felt more secure that way. He hated being alone. He didn't want to die alone. I told him I was pleased that a sergeant would want to travel with a PFC. He said he heard some talk by a few officers that I was—or could be—an asset to any group.

We kept walking, talking, hiding, and firing, when required. We were companions in hell.

Evening approached, and we had to decide where we would spend the night. I noticed a small hill on the border of the woods, facing a large clearing to the front. I told my new friend that this is where we should dig. He wanted to stay at the bottom of the hill, but I convinced him that we should get as close to the top as possible, giving us a clean view of any troops coming toward us. So be it. We dug and dug until we had a good foxhole for the night. We hollowed out a deep hole to live or die in.

I shared my last K-1 ration with my "fox mate," as we huddled in the cold with snow falling. He told me he was a teacher, married, with two children, and I believe he came from Indiana. We talked quietly, cautiously, careful not to get too close. I did tell him that if we ever got back to the States, I would like for us to someday meet each other's families and be friends.

We could hear and see other soldiers digging into our little hill. Soon, there were many other foxholes, running from the base of the hill and moving up toward the top, where we were.

Night fell and with it the temperature kept pace. We were colder, hungrier, and more miserable than the previous day, but we kept hoping for the best—to at least live another day. Again, we huddled up and tried to sleep. Eventually, we dozed off.

As dawn was about to break, the sound of tanks and the movement of troop vehicles in front of our hill roused us from our sleep. The engines' noise was joined by the neighing of horses. Raising myself out of the foxhole for a quick glance, I saw the old World War I artillery pieces being drawn by horses. Alongside were modern guns and tanks, approaching the base of the hill. Our suspicions were confirmed. Hitler was gambling everything for a quick victory.

The Germans stopped and prepared to attack the hill and its many visible foxholes.

Machine guns started to strafe the area with their deadly fifty-caliber messengers of death.

I told the sergeant what I saw. He suddenly decided he wanted to see this for himself. The entire area was under extremely heavy fire, and I yelled, *"No!"*—but it was too late. He foolishly raised his head above the top of the foxhole for just a fraction of a second, but it cost him his life. With a bullet hole in his head, he fell into my arms. What a terrible shame. What a waste of a nice, young man, who so wanted to be with his beloved family once again. I closed his eyes and laid him down for his final rest, to sleep forever.

I knew he was Catholic and, as best as I could, I said the Lord's Prayer. For good measure, I also said a Hebrew prayer for the dead. It couldn't hurt, for I fervently believed we were all brothers, especially at the time of death.

I recalled my father's words, when we were saying our good-byes. "Being in a war, things may get very bad. When all seems lost, you must always remember that you have a family that loves you and needs you, and you must come back to them safe and sound. Above all, at these times, you must remember the S'hma [the Hebrew prayer that is the basis for the Jewish religion]." He continued, "I was in the Russian army, not by choice, and when we were being attacked, I remembered my God, saying over and over the S'hma. I feel I survived, protected by my faith and love for my God."

I kept saying, *"shmei israel adenoi elihenu, adenoi echod."*

Each time I said the prayer, I said it louder and louder. My words were drowned out by the rumble of approaching tanks and the constant gunfire that accompanied the German advance—gunfire that was concentrated on our positions on this small hill.

The machine gunning seemed to stop. I carefully lifted my head enough to see what was happening. The Germans were burying our soldiers in their own foxholes—they had thoughtfully dug their own graves. How convenient. The tanks advanced to each row of foxholes and spun their huge steel tracks, burying alive the GIs inside each and every hole. Those who tried to escape were immediately gunned down.

It was at that exact moment, when I again said the S'hma over and over, louder and louder, that a dense morning fog suddenly appeared, covering the top of my hill. I said, "Thank you, God. I guess you really did hear me." With that, I said good-bye to my dead friend, picked up my rifle and what ammo I had left, and started to crawl out of my hole. The Germans sensed that some soldiers would take advantage of the fog, and the gunfire started again. Bullets were raining all about me. I crawled as fast and as low as possible, reaching the crest of the hill and going down the other side. Out of sight of the Germans, I was able to stand up, stoop low, and run as fast as possible into the nearby woods.

I made it, stopped to catch my breath, and thought about what the past twenty-four hours had done to my life and to all the others in Co. L.

I never saw any of them again.

I was alone, facing an attacking force far superior in numbers and equipment to our decimated army.

The weather was still terrible. Snow, cold, and heavy clouds hung over the entire area. No planes were flying. Our superior air force was grounded.

The same fog that had covered me, allowing me to leave the foxhole, was now dissipating. This allowed the German tanks to continue to bury alive the men left in the foxholes.

I thanked the powers that be that I hadn't been killed, not buried deep in my own foxhole. I continued walking, meeting up with other soldiers. We fought when necessary but mainly tried to keep away from large confrontations. When out of ammo, we got more by taking from the dead. There were hundreds of them. Again, I looked for some K-1 rations among the dead—they were no longer in need of them.

Later that day, I was crossing an open field area. A young GI walked along with me, just to my left. Suddenly, we took fire from a barrage of 88 shells, aimed directly at us. The 88 shells mainly follow a forward trajectory but then veer to the right. The young man on my left took the main force of the explosion and was killed instantly. Much of his remains showered upon me; I was covered with blood and guts. I fell, blown over by the explosion, and experienced ear-splitting shrieking in my head and a loss of hearing.

(That was the beginning of all my hearing problems, which eventually would lead to a cochlear implant in one ear and a special digital hearing aid in the other.)

Dead soldiers were numerous in this area. I found a discarded pack that contained some clothing, and I scavenged until I found enough to change clothes. I stopped at a small creek that had a little running water, tore off all my bloodied, gut-soaked clothes, washed as best as I could with the water and snow, put on "new" clothes, and moved on. Later, I discovered that I did not have my dog tags. They were either blown off by the explosion or dropped when I tried to clean myself and get dressed again. Going back to find them was out of the question. This loss turned out to be for my benefit.

I had no ammo, no food, and no idea where I was or where the American forces were. I couldn't know where the front lines were now or how close I was to the German front.

Later that afternoon, I spotted a concrete pillbox. I then knew I was still in part of the Siegfried line. I decided to try to spend the night in the pillbox, knowing it would offer, at the very least, protection from the constant shelling.

I opened the door to the concrete entrenchment and, to my surprise, I saw five other American soldiers inside. All had the glassy-eyed, forlorn look of frustration. There was nothing anyone could say that would be of any value in this situation.

"Hi, can I join this group?" Not expecting an answer, I merely said thanks and sat down on the concrete floor.

Later, we introduced ourselves, not by name so much but by which outfit we were from. All were from various companies and regiments; none was from my group. Conversation was kept at a minimum. One of the men was a lieutenant. I felt he was the most frightened of the group.

We could do nothing but wait to see what would happen next. Evening was now upon us. I had made up my mind as to what I would do. If still here when dawn broke, I would leave and take my chances at finding the American front lines. Possibly, I could find some group still fighting, latch onto them, and continue to be a part of the battle, hopefully with some guidance. But I never was able to further plan a course of action. Shortly afterward, several German SS troops came into the pillbox, saw us there, raised their rifles, and commanded us to kneel on the ground. We were searched and taken prisoner.

Chapter Four

Prisoner

Our group was held until the morning and then ordered to begin walking to an assembly area where other GI prisoners of war were gathered. The notorious SS officers were the ones in charge of interrogating the captured Americans.

I was waiting in line to be interrogated. In front of me was a young Jewish soldier from New York, with a name like Goldstein. He was asked several questions, and then they looked at his dog tags. The SS officer shouted, "*Sie sind ein Jude.*" (You are a Jew.) He killed him instantly, saying, "*Sie sind jetzt ein guter Jude.*" (You are now a good Jew.)

I was next. "*Schnell, kommen Sie hier.*" (Quickly, come here).

I was about to be interrogated when there was a warning of some kind, calling the officer away. The officer left and the rest of the SS agents were told to march us to another area. There, we were assembled into smaller groups of about fifty to seventy. My group was taken to a nearby farmhouse, still on the fighting front. I could hear the sound of tanks moving and artillery being fired, and I wished I were on the other side of the action with my own people.

Our new home was a large room, probably the living room. We were not given any food or water that day. There were no sleeping facilities. We sat on the floor with no room to lie down. The lucky ones were able to find a wall to at least lean against.

Finally, sleep came and with it, a brief respite from the severe problems and uncertain future we faced.

Morning came. We were all awakened and given some hard bread and a type of grain soup. I was thankful for whatever we got.

There were no bathroom facilities. A pail was kept in the same room. It was always full, and with each use, the overflow formed puddles on the floor. There was no real means for having bowel movements. For me, who was used to having two showers a day, this was hell—but it got worse.

We were all taken outside and assigned an area to dig graves. We were told, "Dig or die." We tried digging using small shovels that were ineffective against the cold, frozen ground. With all our efforts, only a few graves were dug—never enough to bury the thousands of dead American and German soldiers that were in this part of the front. The fruitless digging led to a major decision by the German command. Instead of trying to bury the dead, they brought up some bulldozers and pushed all the dead into large piles on either side of the road. They reminded me of the stone hedges in England, except in place of the stone, there were dead bodies and parts of bodies, piled about four feet high and five feet across. It seemed these "dead hedges" were endless.

The weather was getting a bit warmer, and the odor from the piles of human remains was something one could never forget or want to relive. The scene of decaying body parts and the horrible stench permeated my soul.

After sixty-six years, I can still smell the dead and am still aware of the horrors of war, both of which have been part of me forever, like a bad tattoo—a tattoo stenciled forever onto my soul and mind.

That evening, once again, we were gathered in the same room in the farmhouse. I was able to get a spot by the wall on the far side of the room. About 3:00 a.m., on the second night of being kept as a prisoner on the front, I was awakened by the entry of an SS officer, a lieutenant, dressed in his green uniform and high black boots and carrying his holstered weapon. He stepped over and around several men, and when in the center of the room, he shouted, *"Aufstehen!"*

Nobody moved. Not knowing or understanding German, we all just sat there. *"Aufstehen!"* he shouted again. Still, there was no reaction by the men. *"Aufstehen!"* was shouted for the third time. Getting no response, he drew his Luger, placed it against the head of the closest GI, and fired, killing him instantly.

Suffering from dysentery and hunger and regretting my status as a prisoner of war, I felt I had very little to lose, except, of course, my life. I got up and yelled, "Everybody up … up! This son of a bitch means business. Up!" That command they understood, and everyone rose to their feet.

The SS officer looked to see who'd given the command. He saw me and, with his fingers, bid me to come to him.

"*Kommen Sie hier.*" (Come here.)

I did.

"*Wie heissen Sie?*" (What is your name?)

Max Gendelman, I told him. At this point, my ordinarily brown hair was bleached blond from the sun, a result of my often not wearing a helmet. I have blue eyes and for all intents and purposes, my appearance could be construed as a German. My last name, if spelled with two n's, could be a German name—Gendelmann.

"*Ja, ein guter deutscher Name.*" (Yes, a good German name.) "*Gendelmann, woher kommen Sie?*" (Where do you come from?)

"Milwaukee."

"*Ach mein Gott, Milwaukee ist eine gute deutsche Stadt in America!*" (Oh my God, Milwaukee is a great German city in America.)

"*Ya vol.*" (Yes.)

"*Max, Sie sprechen kein gutes deutsch.*" (Max, you don't speak German too good.)

I just shrugged my shoulders and raised my arms, as if to say, "I know."

"*Das ist das Problem mit den jungen Deutsch-Amerikanern—sie sprechen kein gutes deutsch.*" (That is the trouble with young German Americans—they don't speak the real German language.) "*Max, Sie sind jetzt unser Dolmetscher.*" (Max, you are now our interpreter.)

With that, he turned around and walked away. He left me thinking that on this day, December 20, 1944, in an area near the embattled front lines, I—a Jewish boy—became an interpreter for the German SS troops and was cast as the leader of this group of American GIs. If only they'd known.

The next few days passed. Life became a blur. We were not sure where we were, what our destiny was, or what, if anything, we could possibly do to change the outcome.

Life was miserable, but dying was worse. Some Americans were killed for no apparent reason, except for Germans to exhibit control over captured Americans, the bitter enemy.

We were given work details. The most dangerous work to be done was clearing the roads and fields of mines and debris. Often, the mines found us before we found them.

The fighting front had moved farther away from the area where we were kept. The weather improved. The skies cleared, and with it came the constant bombing and strafing by American and British air forces.

Once again, we had casualties on both sides.

About ten days after capture, I was told to get everyone ready to leave. Where and how we were going, I wasn't told. They had us walking into Germany itself to an area where we then boarded boxcars for a trip deep inland.

To get there, we walked for about seven days. The march of the living to live, but some never finished the long journey. Those too weak to maintain the set pace fell from exhaustion and were shot. Their bodies were pushed over to the side of the road. That was a warning for all to heed. The dead no longer had to bear the brutality of the SS Panzer soldiers. Hopefully, they were at peace.

I was glad to at least get farther away from the front area, which was constantly being strafed by our planes. The future, I thought, would be much better than the recent past. How mistaken I was.

We walked and came to many small German villages. They were farming communities, generally in valleys surrounded by lush countryside. All were quite similar, built near a church, with a main street of stores: a bakery, butcher shop, food, small retail stores—hardware and general merchandise—and an inn. All the villages looked so peaceful, so close but still so far away from the tumult of war.

It became apparent, however, that even these villagers knew their beloved Deutschland was in trouble. Their leader's goal of trying to conquer all of Europe and later the world was in serious trouble. Someone had to take the blame.

As we entered a little village, we saw a large banner stretched across the small road. It read: *"Die Juden sind unser Unglück."* (The Jews are the cause of all of our problems.) They were all so sure of it that they would eventually murder over six million Jews, but it seemed there were still a handful left some place that caused the war to go so poorly.

This same banner stretched across the roads entering and leaving all the villages we walked through, all to bolster the German moral. The villagers came out of their houses and shops to gawk at us and taunt us. Some would throw old fruit or stale bread. We gladly picked these up, if and when the guards were not looking. I believe it made them feel good to see the "defeated Americans." We left each village, but their troubles still remained.

After walking a great distance into Germany, our journey came to an end at a railroad marshaling yard. Those who survived looked forward to a promised rail trip, destination unknown. That was another mistake. If known, we would have gladly continued walking, rather than experience the torture of the next phase of our lives as prisoners of war.

The German boxcar measured ten by thirty feet, with a cargo space of three hundred square feet total. The sides were wooden slats with open spaces between each slat, allowing the cold and wind and snow and rain to refresh its occupants. These cars were built and meant for cattle and pigs of a different kind, not the "American pigs."

All the railroad cars in Germany now had large red crosses painted on their roofs. This was done to keep the American and British air forces from bombing and strafing them. Since the marking of all cars with red crosses abused the symbolic use of that humanitarian symbol, the Allied Forces were justified in destroying the railcars with Red Cross markings. What a shame, for in some instances, where the markings were legitimate, many wounded prisoners of war met their final fate. The decision was correct. The German high command was to blame.

Permit me this brief aside: *Recently, in Naples, Florida, a group of dedicated men, led by a friend, Merill Kuller, financed the purchase of an old boxcar that was used during this period to take Jews to the death camps and later to transport groups like mine to areas deep into Germany. After the car arrived in Miami, on Florida's east coast, they loaded it onto Merill's large sailboat and safely brought their precious symbol of Germany's inhumanity to man, the slaughtering of the "Six Million," to Naples on the west coast. The car was accurately restored to what it actually looked like in 1944 and is now on display in Naples at the exhibit of the Jewish Historical Holocaust Museum.*

Upon dedication of the reconstructed car, a victim and survivor of the holocaust, Mr. Abe Preis, said with tears in his eyes and a voice filled with emotion, "This car is an emblem of Nazi brutality. The devil himself could not have devised such hell."

And so be it. He was right on the button.

We were assembled in groups of about eighty and told to climb aboard. Those who were too weak or did not comply fast enough were shot and their bodies hauled away. When the car was filled to capacity, all standing shoulder to shoulder, the door was slammed shut and locked.

Over the next five days, in our new home, our ordeal in hell started anew. Within a short time, the stench became overpowering. A small leaking pail was our bathroom. The open areas between the wooden slats created a hardship, allowing the cold, harsh, wintery weather to make our lives even more miserable, but at the same time, we were thankful for the fresh air because it offset the vile conditions in the car. Food and water were an afterthought.

Once a day, when the train stopped near a siding, we were all let out. We had an opportunity to try to relieve ourselves, and we were offered our daily ration of food, a dish of soup—borscht—with a single piece of hard bread.

We existed, just barely, but some of our group didn't. We could hear our own planes firing at us, not knowing, of course, which Red Cross-emblazoned cars were legitimate. We were all glad that at the very least, they were now fighting back.

Within the car, those who were hit by the strafing didn't survive very long. No help came for them. The dead were kept with us until the next day, when once again we were let out for a short time. As the *Dolmetscher*, I asked for and was generally given permission to remove the dead and to say a few words, a few prayers, for their passage to the other world. Those who prayed, in their own way, not only prayed for their comrades who didn't make it but also silently gave thanks for being alive, for being—so far—one of the lucky ones.

And so it continued. Night became day, and day later turned to night, bringing with it the cold and dark thoughts of what the future might hold when our journey finally ended. We arrived at our destination, Stalag IV B.

Assembled in a large room, I saw hundreds of American Red Cross boxes stacked against the walls. Heaven would soon be ours!

Shortly after arriving, two British soldiers came in. They had been captured in Dunkirk early in the war and were now spokesmen for the German command at the prison. Apparently, they had become close friends with them too.

As the representative and spokesman for our group, I said, "Gosh, are we glad to see you. Can you see to it that we can get some food and water? I see the American Red Cross parcels. They may have soap, razors, and goodies. Can we get these now?"

"What money do you have to pay for these parcels," asked one of the Brits.

"What the hell are you talking about? These are American parcels, and we are Americans."

"You must have some money or jewelry hidden somewhere, like up your ass."

"Are you kidding," I replied. "My ass has been searched so many times it's like the entrance to a railroad tunnel."

"What a shame. No money, no jewels, no parcels, nothing." With that, the Brits walked out, leaving us wondering whose side these bastards were on now. Later, we found out the British POWs—the ones who were captured early and ran the stalags—went home very wealthy.

Our stay was cut short. We never received any food or drink. We were assembled into smaller groups of about forty to fifty men, loaded onto a military vehicle, and taken to our next "home away from home." We were taken to a *Zuckerfabrik*, a sugar factory in the German village of Dobeln.

So the next phase of my life as a *Gefangener* (prisoner) was about to begin.

Upon arriving in this small village, we were taken to a large barn-type structure. We entered a large room, in the center of which stood a potbellied cast-iron stove—our heating and cooking plant. On one end of the room were wooden bunk beds and on the far end were wooden tables and chairs. Our guard then told me we would be given work duties *"morgen"* (tomorrow morning).

I demanded, *"Mir daffen essen."* (We need something to eat.)

"Morgen," he replied. And with that he left, locking the door.

We then realized we were not alone. Seated at the tables were about twenty-eight Russian prisoners of war, who were about to be served their one precious meal of the day, a bowl of borscht with one piece of dark bread.

A Russian woman, also a POW, was the leader of the group of men. She came up to me, as I was the one who had spoken to the guard. She looked at us—dirty, filthy, unshaven, wearing clothes that beggars would throw away—and tried to converse.

"Do you speak Russian?"

"No."

"Do you speak French?"

"No, do you speak English?"

"Nein, sprechen Sie deutsch?"

"Yah, a bissel."

"Gut." (Good.)

"Wann haben Sie zuletzt gegessen?" (How long has it been since you ate)?

I told her it was so long ago that I couldn't remember. We were all starving.

What happened next is something that I will remember as long as I live.

The young woman then related our situation to her fellow Russians. They all got up from the table, walked across the room, took us by the hand, and escorted us back to their table, giving up their one meal. They divided what they had, so all of us had some of the borsht and a small piece of bread. We were all so thankful. With tears in our eyes, we hugged each one to show them our appreciation.

Considering the atrocious treatment we'd received from the British and the heartwarming reception we received from the Russians, I could not be blamed for thinking that I'd rather fight the British than the Russians. That thought stayed with me for many years.

In the morning, we were given a piece of bread and a light cup of a grain drink, which was tolerable. The men were assigned tasks of picking kohlrabi and processing it into brown sugar. They were able to sneak back some of the brown sugar in their pockets. When placed on a piece of bread and heated on the stove, it formed a very delicious, tasty delicacy—a sugar candy treat that was like heaven on earth.

In the evening, as part of my work assignment as the *Dolmetscher*, I dispensed the borscht using a ladle that measured out how much each man got. Several fellow prisoners resented me for several reasons, mainly because I was Jewish but also because I was friendly with the German guards and didn't work in the fields or factory. I firmly believed that even if I had, they would have found other reasons to resent me as a symbol of designated authority.

To alleviate the grumbling from a few of the men who insisted that I had shorted them on the soup, each night I assigned another person to do the ladling. This should have solved the problem, but it didn't. There was a small click, led by a big Polish lad. The resentment became very open, with taunting remarks as to my cheating him and his close buddies. I was constantly accused of instructing each new man who served the soup to skimp on the portions for these few.

"Hey, Jew boy, are you kissing the Germans' asses? I think you are and sucking their dicks!"

I took the taunts from them, considering the source, but my patience finally came to an end when their taunting took another turn.

"Kike, I know for a fact what you do to your mother. She loves it when her little son does it, with his father watching."

That was enough. That piece of shit crossed the line.

I called for a circle. When there were disagreements, where two guys wanted to fight it out, we would form a circle in the middle of the room and sing very loudly to cover the sounds of the brawl—to make the guards unaware of what was going on.

This guy was happy to finally teach me a lesson and to take over command of the group. "Fine, asshole. I'll knock the shit out of you, and maybe I'll even let you live. Let's fight!" He was about six foot three, weighed approximately 220 pounds, and had arms like a gorilla, so it seemed.

I was only five foot nine and a half and weighed about 180, but I was hard and tough, having developed my strength from years of working in my dad's business, loading and unloading roofing materials and carrying hundred-pound kegs of nails and bundles of galvanized sheet metal. As a freshman at the University of Wisconsin—Madison, I was required to take a course in athletics. Not active in intramural sports when in high school, I was not interested in football, tennis, or wrestling. I chose boxing. I only had one semester of boxing and seemed to be successful at it, winning several of my first matches.

The circle formed. The singing started.

Chris came out charging at me. With his long arms, he landed a few good hard blows to my body and head, and I soon realized that I just couldn't box him—I would never be another Max Bear. Instead, when he next swung at me, I ducked under the swing and hit him with all my might in his stomach, with a left and a right. At the same time, my knee found his groin area. When he doubled up, I brought my head up to meet his jaw, and he started to fall to the floor. I was so furious at the obscene remarks that he made about my mother that I pounced on him, took his head in my hands, and started to pound his head into the concrete. Truthfully, I was not even aware at that moment what I was really doing.

All reason had left me; just hate and revenge ruled my actions. A few men stopped the fight by pulling me off and away from him. He was not in any serious danger, just bloodied, and he had a splitting headache for several days. That seemed to solve a lot of problems. I never was confronted by any of the men again. They had a different respect for the "fighting Jew." That was my first and last circle.

I won the match, but that never really changed their dislike of having me, a Jew, as their spokesman and in charge of the group. My own feelings for the group were strained to the breaking point. I had some worries that one of them might tell the guards I was a Jew. I knew my only security against such a possibility was that if one informed, all of us would be punished, and the informer would be "eliminated." I never would become one of the gang, though. I kept to myself, as I had been doing all along, not wishing to hear the same bullshit about how many women they had known. There were many quarrels among the men. I kept my distance.

One night, I tried to save part of my sugar-coated bread to eat later on in the evening. It gave me something to really look forward to. I hid the bread under my mattress. When I went to retrieve it, I found it had been stolen by my own men, by my own fellow Americans. I had such a hollow feeling deep within me, knowing that the men were continuing to steal, one from the other, one American from another, one POW from another. How naïve I was then, but soon I hardened to the fact that maybe all men are not created equal. Some men have a sense of loyalty and respect for justice and more importantly, respect for one another. Sadly, the goal of these men seemed to be how to screw the other guy and get away with it. The "I" was their religion.

For my part, I knew that if I ever came out of this mess a free man, I would never, ever want to see anyone of my group again.

Although I did not work in the fields, I did do manual labor. Besides ladling the borscht, I was assigned to keep the premises orderly. With the aid of the Russian woman—Maria was her name—I kept our quarters neat and clean.

We were all allowed to take a quick, cold shower once a week, but Maria and I were able to do so more often, sometimes together. That arrangement started innocently enough, without planning. One morning I went to the outhouse where we showered. I entered and saw Maria there, completely naked. I was embarrassed and started to leave, but she came over, took my hand, and said, "Come in. The water's fine." I did so, and this arrangement worked out to be delightful, in most respects. There was no sex involved, just appreciation for each other's company.

She told me many stories about the Russians—about the people, the army, the suffering, the many hundreds of thousands of her compatriots who were killed in battles against the Germans, who betrayed them. The Germans had been their partners. Hitler and Stalin supposedly were friends. That friendship ended, however, when Hitler gave orders to attack and crush Russia, a decision that proved to be the downfall of Hitler and Germany. Russia was too big to be run over like Poland and the other countries. And the cold winter was an ally, which helped to defeat the Germans and their war machine.

The two great errors that Hitler made—not invading England when he had the opportunity, and invading Russia when he should not have—led to his final decision of trying to break through the American armies with the Battle of the Bulge.

Maria and her group were lucky they hadn't been killed when captured. I asked her to tell me about the Russian armament—their rifles, their equipment, and their tanks. I had heard stories about the size and power of the new Russian tanks, of which they were especially proud. They were larger than the Americans' Sherman tanks or the Germans' Tiger.

Several weeks after we arrived, Maria and her fellow prisoners were moved out of our barn in Dobeln. I would love to have gotten more information—her full name, address, family—but that was not to be. Their move out was so fast and unexpected. She and the other kind prisoners were now only a fond memory. I still hope they made it through the rest of the war. I missed the Russians. Their kindness was an experience that I will always cherish.

As the group leader and the *Dolmetscher*, I had some leeway, though I was not permitted to go to the village. One day I decided that I must see what Dobeln looked like. If stopped, I'd say I was checking up on my men in the fields and in the factory.

Dobeln was a nice, clean, typical German village, with the usual bakery, meat and food market, pharmacy, pub, and restaurant. It also had a banner that blamed their troubles on the Jews, and why not? Someone had to be blamed. It was just easier to blame the Jews.

Walking down a side street, I noticed a middle-aged woman sitting on her porch. In an act of friendship, I nodded to her, and our eyes made contact. She then said something to me. Not hearing too well and not understanding what she said, I went up to her. She wanted to know if I was an American prisoner.

"*Ya vol.*" (Yes.)

In my limited knowledge of pure German, she asked me if I was hungry. I answered yes.

"Would you like some tea and some food?"

"Yes, that would be very much appreciated."

"Please come into my house."

I looked around and saw no other people in the area who could see me enter her home. She took my hand and escorted me inside, sitting me down at her kitchen table.

"Please feel comfortable. Take off your jacket, if you wish."

I removed my outer jacket, and then she served me hot tea with a platter of bread, sausages, and strudel. It was heaven.

"Where is your family?" I asked

At that, she started to tell me a sad tale, crying as she did so. Life under the Hitler machine had dealt her a terrible blow. Her husband was killed on the Russian front. She had two sons and believed both were killed fighting on the Western Front near Belgium. She did not blame her loss on the Americans. The blame rested on the Reich.

She started to cry again. I took her hand and tried to console her. She said that I reminded her of her sons, whom she longed to hold once again. At that, she asked if she could hold me. I hesitated but agreed and embraced her in return. She then kissed me, and the second kiss was quite passionate. She took my hand and placed it on her bosom, looked into my eyes and, without saying so, seemed to ask me to love her and help relieve her loneliness.

I was taken aback and very hesitant, knowing that if this went any further and I was apprehended, I would be shot immediately. I lifted her chin and told her it was wrong for me to try to replace her family. It would be too dangerous for both of us. She nodded. I thanked her and left, wondering how many thousands of German women were waiting for their husbands and sons to come back to them. How sad. How lonely. How useless wars really are. How the burden of war also falls on the women who are left behind, crying and waiting and knowing that their waiting will not bring back their loved ones.

Was my dear mother also sitting on her porch, sad and lonely? She had no information as to whether I was living or dead or whether I would ever return to her.

Not hearing and not knowing but expecting the worst news was the hardest burden for parents of young soldiers to bear. Reading the newspapers and hearing the news on the Philco radio, they were only told of the large number of casualties: dead, wounded, or missing. Were the missing part of the dead or possibly prisoners of war?

I could only imagine the grief my family was experiencing.

One morning when my mother was home alone, the postman came up to the front door and rang the bell. She had no sooner opened the door than she saw he had a telegram in his hand, the sort that notified immediate relatives of soldiers killed or missing in action.

My mother became hysterical and shouted, "No! No, you can't give me that! There must be a mistake. My *zinnele* [son] is fine. Go away!" The poor postman kept telling her that she must take the telegram, and she must have faith that all would be well. My mother would not listen and tried to close the door. The postman put his hand in the opening, trying again to have her take the telegram. At that time, my mother bit the postman's hand. In pain, he dropped the telegram onto the floor of the porch and took off to get medical aid. He understood and never made any charges against her.

I was told later that after my parents were informed that I was missing in action, my mother would go to see Rabbi Twerski very often, seeking assurance that I was alive. Was God protecting me?

"Feigel, do you trust me?"

"My dear Rebbe, you know that I do. What a question!"

"Do you take me to be a fool?"

"Of course not."

"Do you know that I write a letter each and every day to our Max?"

"Yes, my Rebbe."

"Then, dear Feigel, don't you see that I know he is alive. For if he were dead, why would I write to him every day?"

I could just picture how he would raise his head to the heavens and ask forgiveness for stretching the truth to fit the situation. After all, what he did and said was a *mitzvah* (a good deed). He had to say something to try to calm my mother, who was on the edge of a nervous breakdown. She always felt much better when she left, thanks to the wise man.

And so it was. About three months after the first telegram came, informing my parents that I was missing in action, the second telegram came, informing them that I was alive and a POW in Germany. The Germans were great record keepers, and to their credit, they did, at times, release the names of prisoners of war.

Rabbi Twerski was again, as usual, correct. My mother showed him the latest telegram, and they both cried unashamedly.

Dobeln was about thirty miles northeast of the great Saxon triangle, which consisted of the large, important cities of Chemnitz, Dresden, and Leipzig. This area was famous for its many universities, hospitals, medical centers, museums, and art colonies. Because it was on higher ground than the cities in the famous triangle, we were able to hear the explosions and see the "fireworks."

By late January and early February 1945, our air force started to establish superiority over the Luftwaffe. In an attempt to bring the Nazi regime to a point where they might want to surrender—or at the very least to weaken the defenses to a point where our armies could more easily advance in the race to reach and conquer Berlin—the triangle was bombed night and day. What a waste. The destruction was brought upon themselves, but I felt this destruction was all for naught.

In addition to bombing the triangle, we could hear the continued warfare to the west, to the area bordered by the Elbe River. Each day the sounds grew closer. We were about ten miles to the east of the Elbe, and each day, with the advance of the fighting toward the river, our hopes grew that before long, we would be liberated—to live once again as free men.

When I estimated that our army might reach our area within a day or two, I called a meeting of our entire group. I tried to tell them what

I thought the situation was but gave them no assurances, as I was only guessing at what was happening. I gave them the following scenario: if the army approached Dobeln, the Germans might just retreat, or they might decide to move us out with them. But if really hard-pressed and seeking some form of revenge, they might decide to kill us all before retreating.

Having laid out the various possibilities, I made this suggestion: "I feel the approaching armies, at the rate it seems they are going, will probably cross the Elbe and reach us within twenty-four to forty-eight hours. Therefore, I feel the need to leave here—to get into the nearby woods and onto higher ground while awaiting our troops. The danger is in not knowing what the Germans will do to us if captured again, and if we do get caught, what the timing might be for rescue. There's no reserve of food, but we've fasted, unwittingly, before."

All agreed to go.

The very next night, which was dark and overcast, we silently took off in single file, leaving our Dobeln home. I led my group into the nearby woods to await our saviors.

We stayed out one day and two nights.

The Americans did not come. The sounds of advancing troops and war—tanks rumbling, artillery spitting out their messengers of death, vehicles and infantry moving, slow and determined, with men facing and cheating death with every step they took—came to a halt. We realized that for some unknown reason, our troops had stopped; in fact, they seemed to be in retreat. I was disheartened. Our men must have been overwhelmed, slaughtered by the Germans.

I was right in my thinking that the Americans should have rescued us by now. They had crossed the Elbe and were on the move toward us and our freedom. Instead, it turned out that Stalin sent President Roosevelt a very stern and threatening message: "Stop your advance. The area east of the Elbe is and will be part of Russia. Get out!" And so the American armies gave in to the Russian demands. They retreated across the Elbe.

On the second day, with no Americans in sight, we were surrounded by an armed German patrol. We had no other course but to surrender and to once again become prisoners of war. We were returned to our barn in Dobeln. For some unknown reason, we were not killed or severely reprimanded, other than being told there would never be a next time and slapping a red triangle on our backs, indicating we each had tried to escape. The previous guards were transferred out and new guards assigned. I guessed the members of our group were good workers, and good workers were badly needed.

I got to be friendly with a new guard, an old man who had the night shift. By this time, all available fighting men were on the front lines. Guard duties were handled by men not fit to fight, although they carried loaded rifles and were taught how to shoot. My guard's name was Moshe, or at least that's what I called him. He seemed like a nice, elderly Jewish grandfather. We got along by respecting each other and by not taking advantage of any situation, which would cast him or me in a bad light. That paid off.

On April 13, 1944, Moshe came to me and said in German, "Max, I have some sad news for you. I'm sorry to have to tell you that your president, Franklin Delano Roosevelt, has died." At first, I thought he was taunting me, but after looking deeply into his eyes, I realized that it was true.

The Roosevelt era had ended. He had died without seeing the end to this terrible war, World War II.

Days passed, but my desire to escape did not. One night, I woke up in a sweat, silently crying. As usual, I'd been dreaming of home, my family, and the great food my mother always made for us, but I could not remember what my mother looked like during that dream. I was trembling and knew then that come what may, I must try once more to get to the American army at the Elbe. I could not have another dream like that while in captivity.

This time I would not take my entire group. I really wanted to go alone, but I felt it was my duty to explain to the men what my plan and intentions were. That night, I called a meeting and told them that I would be leaving them. They would be okay. My trying to escape should not have a punitive effect on those remaining.

To my surprise, quite a few wanted to go with me, but I had to limit the group to about ten. I did this by presenting a very dark picture of probable success. I told them I was going to a different route to make it all the way to the Elbe. The number of men who finally wanted to go with me was reduced to eight.

I presented my plan to the group and gave them a final chance to back out, if they so desired. None did. They told me that even though we didn't always see things in the same light, they felt I was a fair and good leader. That was good to hear. I then laid out the details. We would travel west to get to the Elbe. We would travel only at night. We would try to bypass any village or farming community and be guided by electric power lines that were usually on the outskirts of the villages. We would track the lines in a westerly direction. We had no food but I felt that within two to three days at the most, we should be able to meet the Americans. On or about April 16, four months after the great battle started, we took off. It was my second try for freedom.

These four months had changed my entire life—months of starvation, constant bouts of dysentery and vomiting, unsanitary conditions, and soiled clothing. I existed but barely. At least I was still alive. So many others couldn't say the same, lying nameless in some grave or rotting in a hedgerow of bodies.

My plan was working. I located a power line to follow. We traveled slowly at night and found deep cover to spend the daylight hours. The next few nights were clear, with a moon to give us enough light. Although the weather was cool, it was dry. We didn't have the problem of deep snow, rain, or bitterly cold temperatures.

We were lucky in spotting and avoiding several German patrols. They were not looking for us or for anything. They seemed to want to finish their patrol and get back to their warm barracks.

Air attacks continued in this area, but they were directed at the triangle and troop concentrations. I felt it was a good sign. The area to our east was constantly bombarded. Maybe the Germans would pull back, allowing the Americans to at least control the area on both sides of the Elbe.

We spent two nights traveling slowly toward the Elbe. We were getting closer, as we heard and saw air attacks and constant artillery barrages covering the area where we planned to go. Being so close, we now had to advance slowly by day. Later that day, we came over a hill and were able to see the River Elbe.

I was disheartened to see the Americans were still on the other side, having made no attempt to cross and advance. We were not aware of the agreement that Stalin was able to wrench out of President Roosevelt. Freedom seemed so elusive again.

I told my small group that several choices were available to them. Stay where they were now—but for how long, I could not say; turn around and head back to Dobeln; or try to reach the Elbe and, hopefully, a rescue. This final choice was the most dangerous of the three.

I was asked what I would do. I told them I intended to go toward the Elbe, come what may. All decided to go with me—bravely, foolishly, or just ill-advised by a Jewish sniper turned leader. We left the hill and started to walk as fast as we could toward the Elbe and the Americans.

Here is where our luck turned.

The Germans saw us and laid down a barrage of 88 shells.

The Americans saw us, thinking we were a German patrol, and they started to shell us as well, using deadly phosphorous projectiles. If you were hit with a phosphorous shell, the chemical burned and penetrated the skin, very deep and very deadly.

We managed to find some security in a depression on the ground, caught in between two combatants. The Germans knew who we were. The Americans thought we were Germans. Once again, I kept repeating the S'hma. It had worked before. Maybe it would work again.

I had a white cloth and tried to wave it as high above my head as possible, while still having some ground cover. That was only partially successful. The Germans stopped their shelling, but the Americans continued for a while longer. They also finally stopped.

When darkness fell, the Germans sent out an armed patrol to pick us up. Once again, I became the *Dolmetscher* and explained as best as I could how happy we were to see them. I told them we got separated from our main group. We had been part of a detail working in the woods, got lost, and were trying to get back to Dobeln. I guessed that we just turned the wrong way. Could they please get us back to our group?

I wasn't sure they believed my cock-and-bull story, but we were told to follow them and walk away from the front. One of the men in our group had a leg wound and couldn't walk. I got a few men to lift him onto my back, and with his arms around my neck and his legs around my waist, I started walking, step by step, away from the front. Two German guards were assigned the task of escorting us back to Dobeln. And again we were surprised and thankful we were not killed.

The others took over carrying the wounded guy by fashioning a makeshift sling from their jackets, and we all took turns in the carrying and caring.

Traveling in the daylight, it didn't take long to get back to our barn in Dobeln. We were very apprehensive as to the greeting we would receive upon our arrival. Moshe met us. He told the two guards who escorted us that he would take over, and they could go back to their outfit. He read us the riot act—but with a twinkle in his eye. We were still friends. I trusted him, shook his hand and, in the best German possible, I made him a promise. If I lived through this and ever had the opportunity, I would come back to Dobeln to look for him and help him in any way possible.

I was not able to keep my promise to my friend Moshe. Shortly afterward, we were assigned a new guard. I was told that Moshe got very sick and was in very serious condition. That may have been so, but I had the haunting feeling that my dear old friend was punished for having let us escape again. I was struck with the ever-present thought that my "friends" all seemed to die or leave me. Moshe was a friend I would never forget.

A question was always in the forefront: "Why did they not kill us for trying to escape, not once but twice?"

Being Jewish and understanding and speaking German poorly were advantages that so far had saved my life. Plus, I believed the S'hma helped. But the real answer behind our not being shot became apparent very shortly. With Russian armies getting closer, the decision had been made to move our group to a safer area and prepare us for our next assignment in the mountains of Czechoslovakia. Our group would have the esteemed honor of continuing to work for the new republic.

After a two-day trip, on foot and by truck, we arrived in Linda, Germany, a very small farming village near the border of Czechoslovakia. Once again, our group of about fifty was housed in a large barn, which had an adjoining field that was surrounded by a barbed-wire fence. I learned this was all part of the Fischer farm, a small, beautiful farm that was the pride of the Fischer family for many generations. The German army forcibly took over a part of the farm and the barn to make it into a makeshift prison to house the POWs.

Spring was upon us, and the weather was much better. Springtime in Germany—oh my! Whoever thought I would be here to enjoy the weather and scenery? What a vacation, and all at the expense of my hosts, the Nazis.

I spent as much time as permitted walking along the fenced perimeter and wondering if this war would ever come to an end—and if so, would we be alive to experience freedom once again? What did the immediate future hold for us? What did it hold for me? Always the same thoughts, the same questions.

During some of my constant walking along the fence lines, I saw a young German lieutenant wearing a sling, seemingly to protect an injured arm. He was a rather handsome young man, about twenty years old, with typical Teutonic features: blond hair, light complexion, and blue eyes that shined and seemed to pierce right through you. I guessed he was about my height and stature. I nodded to him, making eye contact, and kept on walking.

Chapter Five

An Unlikely Meeting

I was on my "fence route" the very next day and again, I saw the young lieutenant. He looked at me. I nodded once more and motioned for him to come closer, saying, "*Guten Morgen.*" (Good morning.)

He acknowledged me with a clearly spoken "Thank you."

"You speak English?"

"Yes, of course. We all learn English in our schools."

"Where were you hurt?"

"I was shot down over Russia and am lucky to be alive. I am recovering on my grandmother's farm."

"My name is Max Gendelman. I come from a city in America called Milwaukee, a good German city."

"Yes, we all know about Milwaukee. My name is Karl Kirschner. My grandparents name is Fischer, my mother's parents. They own this farm."

He was neatly dressed, clean-shaven, and very respectable. In sharp contrast, I was in my dirty clothes, with a long red beard, unshaven since mid-December. Still, in spite of my appearance, I felt I was an equal to this German lieutenant. My parents had taught me to feel proud of who I was, no matter the situation. And there was no better place to test one's self-assurance than in the army. I had learned back in basic training to not take shit from anyone. I held my head up high.

The following day, I took up my vigil, walking and waiting near the outer perimeter of the fenced-in area of our prison farm, the same spot where Karl and I had talked. I wondered if I would see him again.

He did not disappoint me. We greeted each other, had some small talk, and then he asked me, "Max, do you play chess?"

"I do."

"Would you like to play chess with me?"

I was really taken aback by that simple but far-reaching request.

"Yes, Karl. How would I be able to play chess with you?"

"Max, if you promise not to cause trouble for me, I would be honored to arrange a way to have you meet with me late tonight about midnight. We can play chess in my loft, in the barn nearby."

I assured him that the honor would be mine, and that I would never cause any problem that would hurt him in any way.

"Good. At midnight, the guards retire. You will meet me here. I will lift the corner of the fence just high enough for you to crawl through. We can then play for a few hours before you have to return. *Gut?*" (Good?)

"*Ya vol, gutte.*" (Yes, good.)

For the rest of the day I was nervous but excited at the thought of the clandestine arrangement. Could this whole meeting be just a trap? But why? Perhaps Karl was really another Nazi officer, wishing to entice a POW into trying to escape. No, I felt confident. If the entire meeting was a disaster, he too would be in danger.

Still not sure if this chance for a few hours of partial freedom would actually take place, I put on my dark outfit—the only clothes I had—and at midnight, I was at the appointed spot. I heard a whisper.

"Max?"

"Karl?" I answered.

The barbed wire and fence was then silently lifted and, getting as close to the ground as possible, I crawled under and through. Karl then dropped the fence to its normal position. He took my hand to guide me in the dark to the nearby barn. We climbed a ladder to reach his room in the upper loft. I felt I had climbed the ladder to heaven.

"Max, my mother and my grandmother both know and approve of our meeting. My grandmother has prepared some sandwiches for you. I also have cognac that I saved for a special occasion and a few good cigars for us to enjoy."

I stared in amazement. Nothing that I could have said would have adequately expressed my deep feelings of appreciation. This moment was mine to experience, to cherish, and to remember for as long as I lived, however long that would be.

"So let's eat, and drink, and play chess."

I had to ask myself if this was real, after enduring four months of hell, starving, and constantly facing but miraculously avoiding death, and bearing the burden and sadness of so many of my fellow soldiers having died. This could be real or a scene in some movie, created by imaginative writers. To me, it had to be real—proof of which was my being here, alive, and with Karl. But if it was not reality and only a dream created by my own desires and imagination, when would it end? And where would I be when I awoke?

I greedily devoured the wonderful sausage and egg sandwiches, and with hot coffee, I started to feel human again.

"Max, I want to be your friend. You must trust me."

"Karl, I do trust you. I do so as a friend to friend."

A reporter long after the war asked me if it ever seemed strange to have befriended a so-called enemy. But it was never about "the enemy" between Karl and me; it wasn't about the uniforms we wore. If I had felt Karl was a true Nazi, we would not have become friends—and thank God, Karl didn't see me as a threat either. And maybe it had to do with our ages. I was twenty-one; he was nineteen. Maybe we were naïve but more than that, we were able to be truthful with our own feelings. And the truth was simple. We saw in each other an immediate connection, a brother.

But in that moment, I was feeling much more philosophical about the human condition and our condition. I felt a release of everything I had been thinking, and I said, "Karl, it is not right for two nations to have war, to force men to kill one another. It is not right for one nation to create an environment and situations where war is deemed necessary. One nation should not take over and destroy other nations. Germans and Americans are mostly good people who live and love and eat and sleep and have wonderful families. We were not born to grow into manhood and face the task of killing other human beings or to die in battle on some foreign land. I do not cherish the thought that I had to kill, and

I'm sure that most German soldiers also feel the same. Could we shake hands, not as two forlorn soldiers on a field of battle but as two young men, cast together by some unseen force, who respect each other as individuals and who long for friendship and peace?"

I put out my hand. Karl took it, and we both shook hands; we saluted each other, drank our cognac, and vowed for a long and true friendship.

At this, we turned to the chessboard.

Karl was a fair player, but I was just a little bit better, having been on the chess team for our high school, North Division High School in Milwaukee. It did not take long, and I was able to win the match. Karl looked unhappy, so I suggested that we play another game. This time I managed to lose. We were now even. Karl and I both felt better; Karl was happier and more relaxed. We talked for several hours, finished the food, cut deeply into the cognac, and lingered over a great cigar. I was never a cigar smoker, but under these conditions, I cherished the opportunity to partake in that pleasure. Dawn was about to break, and we had to prepare to leave so that I could crawl back to reality.

Karl asked, "Can we meet again tonight? Same time, same place?"

"It would be my pleasure. One favor—would it be too much of a problem to ask your grandma for some more of the sausage sandwiches?"

Karl was smiling and said, "No problem. Until tonight. *Gute Nacht, guten Tag.*" (Good night, good day.)

I was in a daze for the rest of the following day. So many thoughts were whirling through my mind. I realized that if we were caught, both of us would be in terrible trouble. He could say he was trying to get some valuable information from me. That might save him, but I would probably be shot on the spot. I weighed the consequences, only to come up with the same answer: go see Karl and partake of the sausages, cognac, cigar, and partial freedom. Yes, the sausages won out. There was no question that at midnight, I would once again be at the fence.

The second evening meeting was even better. We did not play chess; we just talked. And Grandma had made a few German delicacies, including fried potato dumplings (*knishes*) and several kinds of sausages. I was in heaven again. Like all the other German soldiers, I assumed Karl knew me as being of German ancestry—Gendelmann (with two n's) was a good German name. I told him of life in Milwaukee and about the many famous German restaurants, the large beer halls, and the diverse ethnic population that made up this wonderful city. Milwaukee, the beer city of America; and Schlitz, the beer that made Milwaukee famous. I told him how, in the summer, people wore white suits. He said it had been such a long time since he had seen men and women properly dressed.

I asked Karl about himself.

He told me he was born on August 19, 1925, in Freiberg, a medieval German town with old walls surrounding the outskirts. His mother's name was Susie, and she spent most of her time during the week in Freiberg, about ten miles away. On weekends, she brought Karl and the rest of the family here to Linda, while she helped his grandmother with the many farm chores.

"I love being at Linda," Karl said, "walking in the hills and helping with the cows on the farm. I've always spent most of my free time here. I love these old buildings—they were built in the sixteenth century—especially this hay barn with its huge, thick stone walls. There's a little mysterious room where I once found an antique spinning wheel, which my parents later sent to my aunt in America."

Karl's father's name was Rudolph. He was the only one of his family to remain in Germany. He had lost his parents very early in life, and two of his three siblings—a brother and a sister—had gone to America decades earlier and settled in New Jersey. But it was his father's other brother who was Karl's true hero. I watched Karl become animated just speaking about him.

"I really look up to Uncle Fritz; I adore him. He is my idol. He became a petroleum scout for Royal Dutch Shell in the 1920s in the frontiers of Mexico. He was a geologist by training and later discovered a silver mine near Potosi. At that time, he was one of the very few gringos in Mexico. Max, here's a good story.

"During the Mexican Revolution, Uncle Fritz was captured by Pancho Villa's men. They thought he was a spy and sentenced him to death. He was buried in the desert with only his head showing above ground. His face was rubbed with horsemeat and honey, and he was left there in the hot sun to be eaten by coyotes and other animals in the area. After the soldiers left, he kept screaming, hoping against hope that someone would help him. It so happened that two Mexican women were nearby, heard his pleas, and saved his life. They dug him out, and he later married one of the women, Carmen.

"He lived in a village called Teziutlán, east of Mexico City and near the volcanoes. He started a coat hanger factory there. He was loved by the people in the village. They called him *Don Federico*."

Karl's father had been both an elementary and a secondary school teacher; he taught biology. And in order for him to continue to teach, Karl explained, he had to join the Nazi Party. His voice trailed off.

We could hear a faraway rumble, the sounds of war. The Russians were getting closer to Linda, close to the border with Czechoslovakia. The ground shook with the movement of the heavy Russian tanks.

Karl asked me, "Do you know what the rumble is?"

"Yes, Karl. The Russian tanks, hundreds of them, are on the move. They are getting closer. I would guess that they are about thirty-five to forty miles away—I forgot you use kilometers. They are about sixty to sixty-five kilometers away."

"What do you know about the Russian military?"

"Quite a lot. For a time, as a prisoner I was kept with a group of Russian prisoners. They always spoke of their military capabilities and were especially proud of their huge tanks that dwarfed our biggest tanks. When all the tanks moved, the ground would shake for many kilometers."

"Do you know what would happen if they captured a German officer?"

At that, I looked my new friend in his eyes and said, "Karl, if you, a German Luftwaffe officer and pilot, were to be captured, they would certainly question you harshly, and then, at the very least, before probably shooting you, they would cut off your balls and then start cutting a bit higher."

Karl was very quiet. The night was fleeting. The food was already consumed, and the cognac was having its effect when he said, "Let's meet tomorrow. I have a lot of thinking to do. *Gute Nacht*, dear friend."

"*Ya vol, Gute Nacht.*"

I once again left the loft, where I had moments of freedom, to again crawl back into captivity. The sharp contrast was starting to wear on me emotionally.

During the day, I tried to stay away from the group, avoiding the constant, meaningless chitchat. There were, of course, some exceptions—some were above the typical cut of GI. I kept wondering how and why we were selected to be taken to this makeshift prison camp. An occasion arose where I had a chance to get into a conversation with one of the German guards. He seemed friendly enough. After the usual greetings, I asked him too if he had ever heard of the American city Milwaukee. It had become part of my script, being a Jew in Germany and all.

"Jawohl, eine gute deutsche Stadt." (Oh yes, a good German city.)

I related how there were many German bund members in America who were hoping for a German victory, always loyal to the Fatherland.

He then inadvertently let it be known that there always would be a German Third Reich. For deep in the mountains of Czechoslovakia was the huge facility, where the German government would be safe from American bombs. Here, the government would continue to function and eventually rise again to recapture all of its rightful land and its place in the world order.

Now, I finally understood why we were here in Linda; why I was still alive. We were needed as slave labor—to do the dirty jobs that were beneath the German soldiers, to maintain the underground German government facility. There was the echo of *Deutschland über Alles* (Germany above all)—the battle cry for building the "master race."

I realized that if we were moved underground, freedom would be far away. A cold shiver crept up on me. I thought of Karl and longed for the day to turn to night, so that the third meeting could take place.

I heard the welcome greeting, "Max."

"Gute Nacht, Karl." And when the fence and barbed wire were lifted, I eagerly crawled under it.

In the loft, the delicious odor and sight of his grandmother's prepared foods—heaven on earth, almost as good as what my mother always made for me—greeted me. I washed down the food with a beer and started a new cigar. Then we talked.

The background rumble of oncoming tanks, mingling with the slight movement in the ground, confirmed that tanks were definitely on the move and coming increasingly closer to our position on the border.

"Max, I have given my situation a lot of thought. I talked to my mom and told her that I didn't think I would be able to survive here much longer. So what are we going to do about it?"

"Karl, I hear you. But what is this 'we' shit?"

"Well, we are going to do something together, aren't we? You and I must leave here very soon. As far as the German military is concerned, I am a defector, and you have two red triangles on your back that you told me indicate you've been caught twice. They will shoot you on first sight. Max, I know the terrain here and can navigate these hills and woods. With luck, we will get through the German lines before the Russians arrive, and you will help me get to the right people on the American side."

I kept looking at my friend and did not say anything for quite some time. I was thinking of some of the consequences of what Karl wanted and weighed the options available to him and to me. He knew he had to get away from the oncoming Russians, but where to go and how soon? He could leave the farm and go farther inland, hiding in the chaos of the German army's losing battle of trying to defend Berlin. Would he be safer there, only to again await the oncoming Russians? The answer soon became obvious. If Karl could become a "friendly ward of the Americans," he would have the best chance of surviving. I believed that if we could reach the American lines, I would be able to front for Karl. I would explain how he helped me and should be protected as well as possible, considering that the war was still being fought.

Finally, I answered.

"Karl, I'm in favor of working out such a plan. But first you need to get a gun and ammunition for me to carry. Also, in case we're stopped by the Germans, we need some documents that would explain why I'm with you, and we need clothes to cover my American field jacket, two bicycles, some food, water, and a map of the area so we can plot a course toward the American lines."

"Yes, Max. I've also made a similar list, and I can get all this together."

We were lying on the floor, not saying anything, just smoking and thinking about what we were about to do. I finally said, "Now listen carefully. This may be the hardest part in your decision to escape with me. Karl, I never ever intentionally lied to you, but I need to tell you something very important. I told you that my name is Gendelman, a German-sounding name."

"Yes, I know."

"Well, here's the problem. I am not German. I am an American. I am also of Jewish ancestry. Being Jewish, I am not liked by the Germans or by many of my fellow Americans. Jews are killed in Germany, and when captured, if Jewish, they are shot immediately. You would or could be under suspicion for escaping with a Jew. The penalty could be very severe."

Karl was quiet for a long time. He turned and looked me in the eyes and said, "It makes no difference."

Later he said, "Max, I've felt for some time that you were not German but Jewish. You are too smart a man to speak German so poorly. It does not matter to me what your religion is or what your beliefs are, only that you respect me as much as I respect you. After all is said and done, the reality must be faced that we may not survive our attempt to reach freedom. I am content in knowing and feeling that I have made a good lifelong friend in you, regardless of how long that life is, and I feel sure that you must feel the same. Our friendship and our strong-willed desire for freedom will see us through."

There was a pause. I took Karl's hands into mine, swallowed hard, and said, "Yes, thank you."

"Remember how I had told you that my father was a teacher. He was a kind, brilliant, soft-hearted, tolerant man who loved Germany, but he could not abide what was happening to his beloved country. The advent of *Kristallnacht* and the start of the persecution of the German Jews, many of whom were his old friends and students, troubled him deeply. He was ordered to stop teaching anyone Jewish and to report them to a special office. He stopped teaching Jewish students in the school but never reported any of them. He would still teach them at our home. He was caught doing this and reprimanded. He lost his right to teach and was forced to enter the German army. He also lost his pension and was lucky to be left alive. My father was forlorn, but he knew he did the right thing, even considering the harsh penalties that were imposed on him. So you see, once again, we have so much in common. Do you agree?"

"Karl, I do agree. Whatever happens, we are one."

He put his arms around me and hugged me. I embraced him in return. The agreement was cast; no turning back.

Plans had to be defined and preparations started. The hours sped by. I needed to get back to the camp. At the fence, with tears in my eyes, I bid Karl good night. "*Gute nacht, liebe Karl. Bis zum morgen, adieu.*"

The fence and barbed wire were lifted, and I crawled under and through yet again. This time, however, there was someone waiting for me. I couldn't make out who he was in the dark. Not knowing what to expect, I just said, "Hello, aren't you out late?"

"Not as late as you have been the past several nights."

"Who are you? What is your name? What do you want? Why are you spying on me?"

"Relax. I'm not here to spy on you. I'm just here to make sure that when you and your German friend take off, I'm there with you. My name is Nick Grano. I come from Euclid, Ohio. Don't forget my name, Max. I'll always remember yours, because you are going to take me with you to freedom."

At first, I denied that we were going to try to escape. That didn't work. Then I told Nick that it was not my decision. The plan was strictly Karl's, and I could not ask him to take others along at this stage of his planning.

"Enough of this bullshit. You and your German friend have a choice. You take me with you, or as soon as you take off, I'll call the guards. How far do you think you'll get? I don't want to spoil your plans. Please understand, I just want to get away from here."

"Nick, I'll talk to Karl and get you an answer. If we take you, you will have to understand that we call the shots, not you. If you cause any problems or create any disturbances that could cause our mission to fail, I will kill you. And if we do escape and finally reach safety, you will owe me a marker that someday I may have to call. Do you agree?"

"Yes, we have a deal. I won't be a problem, believe me."

"Nick, the final decision will be with Karl, not with me. We will see. I will explain the situation and suggest you also come along."

Preparations for the original plan went forward without my help. Being incarcerated, I really couldn't do much. Karl told his mother and his grandparents what his plans were. He told them he loved them dearly but had to try to leave Germany and get away from the oncoming Russians. They worried but agreed that the risk was worthwhile. Staying and waiting for the arrival of the Russians was not acceptable.

Papers, clothing, two bicycles, and a gun were gathered. His mother and grandmother made and packaged food that would not spoil and that could be easily carried. The bottles of water were packed into the saddlebags of the bikes. A map with the latest information as to the location of the German-American front was marked; our route planned. We were all set to go that night before dawn.

When the fence was lifted, I crawled under and then told Karl another person had to join us. Nick too crawled under, faced Karl, and after we walked away from the fence line, he introduced himself. I explained that we had to take him with us or else scratch the plans—at least for a while. But we all knew time was not on our side. Karl really had no choice.

Cousin Werner and Karl (on right)

Max with his sister Esther, 1928

Max and Karl, pre-WWII

Karl with parents, 1939

Max with parents, c.1943

Karl and father

Max and father

Gasthof Linda

Karl, glider pilot

Karl recovering in hospital, 1945

Chapter Six

Escape

It was time to leave.

Karl's grandmother, all of five feet tall, came over to me. She was a lovely old lady—ruler of the Fischer clan – who, according to Karl's stories, was tough yet kind. In a heavy German dialect that I was barely able to understand, she said, "Max, we trust you to take care of our Karl. Please keep him safe and you too. We love him so much, and he cares so much for you." She lifted her hands to reach my face. I bent down to her. She gave me a long kiss, and then with tears in her eyes, she said, "May God be with you. Please, please, take care of Karl."

I gave her a hug, kissed her, and in broken German, I said, "Frau Fischer, I promise I will take good care of Karl. With God's help, you will all be together again."

With the night soon to give way to the dawn, we said our final good-byes.

I couldn't help but think that this was truly a very strange occurrence. Germans were responsible for the execution of so many Jews—millions of them—yet here, deep in Germany, a German family was pleading for a Jewish American soldier, a prisoner of war, to protect and keep safe a German officer, their Karl. A good, warm feeling crept over me; a feeling that things might change for the good. Strange things do and can happen.

The sky was starting to become lighter as we left Linda. We were a strange trio—two men on bicycles and one man walking alongside.

Karl was dressed in his officer's uniform. He had rolled up a raincoat I had given him that he could put on once we were near to the American line. Nick and I wore old German-style overcoats over our dirty and torn American field jackets. We had worn these jackets constantly since early December, before the start of "the Bulge." It was now about April 25. So much had happened since.

I took turns walking and riding the bicycle with Nick. He was short, about five foot eight, and stout, strong, and good-looking. I got to know a little more about him. He came from a devoted, large Italian family. Our conversation remained rather basic, not getting into any serious in-depth discussions. That suited us both fine. He was a nice young man who was glad to be with us. He did what we asked and seemed to appreciate the attempts we were making to reach freedom.

Our first day was fairly successful. We were very careful traveling around all villages and going off the roads and pathways when we thought we would encounter any patrols.

We would go into a forest or woods to eat and rest.

We headed into the Ore Mountains, which was a wooded area between what was then Czechoslovakia and Germany, with Karl leading the way. He said we would have to go west somehow, but it would be too risky to head directly into the industrial part of Saxony. Off in the distance in the hills, we saw a huge old castle. I thought it looked like a Roman fort, and as I steered our path far away, I wonder what wonderful stories the castle had to tell—stories of wars, of rules, of loves. *Who knows? Maybe I will get to see this castle again*, I thought. But in the meantime, we needed to get the hell out of there.

Later that first day, we were surprised by a small working patrol. Karl was a good actor. He started a conversation, asking them about their duties, where their base was, and how far away the enemy lines were. He said he was escorting two prisoners to a base camp. After some more questioning, they wished him luck. Karl bid them good-bye. We took off, not looking back.

The first night we slept deep in the woods. We ate a nice "grandma meal," thankful for our luck so far. We made our bed among the leaves at the base of some large trees and tried to get some much-needed sleep.

With my mind racing, sleep was delayed. I kept wondering what the next day would bring. Finally, sleep did take over.

At first, we had thought of traveling only at night but soon decided that would really be more dangerous if apprehended. Why would a German officer travel with two prisoners in the dark? That question would be too difficult to answer and to convince any patrol leader if stopped.

Karl was concerned because Nick wouldn't sleep deep in the woods with us. He would find a large tree to sit under, or if he saw a barn, he would try to enter and sleep there. Karl had to put a stop to that, because it was dangerous and foolhardy, endangering all our lives. It turned out Nick was afraid of the dark. We tried to quiet his fears.

When daylight came, we started our journey again. We knew that we were getting closer to the front and the fighting. The sounds of war—the bombings, the tanks, the artillery—were heard in the distance, and airplanes were seen in the area.

Unexpectedly, out of nowhere, a middle-aged German officer on a very large horse rode directly toward us. He was as surprised to see us as we were to see him. "Who are you? What are you doing here?" he demanded.

Karl answered that he was escorting two prisoners to the next compound when his vehicle broke down, out of petrol. Quietly, I reached into my pocket where I kept the gun and unlocked the safety. I was prepared to shoot him.

Suddenly, there was a huge explosion. *"Ach mein Gott!* They are blowing up my tanks! We too are out of petrol, and I don't want them to fall into the hands of the Russians."

With that, he wheeled his horse around, shouted a good wish for Karl, and galloped away toward his tanks in the woods. I gave a deep sigh, thankful I would not have to kill another German.

About noon, we were apprehended by a German scouting patrol that seemed to come out of nowhere. We had been on the alert for patrols, but this one we missed. Karl was questioned and papers shown. We hoped to be let go, but it was not to be. The officer in charge of the patrol was dubious as to why a Luftwaffe officer was escorting two prisoners so close to the front. He instructed us to follow them, under guard with rifles drawn, to a nearby police station. There, we were to be questioned again in order to determine the true story. Escorted into another room, we awaited the commandant's arrival. Suddenly, there was the loud, blaring warning of air raid sirens. Enemy planes could be heard in the distance, and they were getting closer. The German officer told Karl to get into the air raid shelter, fast. They all left the room, running to a nearby underground shelter. When they left, Karl picked up the papers from the desk, and we took off running. We picked up our two bikes, which were near the front door, and ran as fast as possible into the nearby woods. Bombs were starting to fall. Ack-ack guns were firing at the oncoming airplanes. I was thankful for the raid, but afraid we might be killed by "friendly fire."

Bombs fell everywhere, with emphasis on the police and army barracks. We were able to see a direct hit on the station, which we had just vacated. Our luck was certainly holding but for how much longer? A few more moments in the station would have spelled death for us all. I gave silent thanks to my God. He had been so helpful to me—so far, so good. He got an A for his effort and an A-plus for the results.

Unscathed and thankful, we continued again but more cautious than before. We stopped traveling long before dusk. The sounds of war were closer, and we didn't want to get to the front as daylight faded.

The morning of the third day came bright and clear. We felt we were very, very close to the front. I suggested that we ditch the bikes and our backpacks; since our food was already eaten, we had only the water to carry.

"Karl, today is our day. If we are alive tonight, we have a good chance that all will be successful. Nick, if you can pray in Latin, do so. Your pope at the Vatican may have a few good words for our safety."

We had traveled about a mile on a small paved road and just had crested the hill when I saw an American 4x4 half-track with its 50-caliber machine gun. I shouted, "The stars! The stars!" I put Karl on my shoulders and raced forward about fifty yards.

The GIs in the mobile unit had also seen us. To their eyes, we were a three-man German patrol. The machine gun was raised and pointed at us. I yelled at Karl to get down and to Nick to throw off his overcoat. I did likewise.

I ran down the hill toward the half-track and its raised machine gun. Silently, I prayed, "God, please don't let them shoot us."

Then I yelled, "Don't shoot! Don't shoot! We are Americans! Don't shoot! We are GIs. Yankees! We just escaped from a German prisoner of war camp! POWs!"

The officer in the half-track understood. He gave orders for the gun to be lowered.

I was the first to reach them and unashamedly hugged the officer and thanked him.

It took quite some time to have them fully understand the entire scene that they had just witnessed. Nick and I gave them our army serial numbers and assured them that we were not the enemy, nor were we turncoats. Convincing them of Karl's intentions was another matter. The officer made a few calls, and we were asked to get into the half-track. We were then escorted to a command center nearby.

Once in the command area, we were transferred to other officers and told our stories several more times. They separated the three of us and interrogated us separately, to make certain our stories were the same. I finally convinced them that Karl was a hero, not an enemy. They did believe me. With the war still waging, the commanding officer could promise only that he would do everything possible to ensure Karl was treated properly and taken out of the front area. However, we each had to go in a different direction, and Karl and I were separated.

Karl and I spent a few moments together. I explained what had been promised. He would be taken to the rear area to be questioned again, and if all was approved, he would be transported to Belgium for safekeeping, not as a prisoner but as a friend. We hugged and exchanged a kiss on the cheek, and I pledged to keep in touch and to meet again as soon as possible. Karl was then escorted away by two American soldiers.

Nick and I were put into a jeep and taken to an area away from the front. Upon our arrival, we were able to have a hot shower. We were also given clean clothes and a meal fit for a king—certainly fit for a hungry former POW.

My first night in five months spent as a free man. Before I retired, I once again recited the S'hma, gave thanks to the Almighty, and thought of my beloved parents. I was safe, but how long would it take for them to know that? I could only imagine the grief and sorrow they were still experiencing. I vowed that someday I would make up the terrible sad days with good and happy ones. I would give them *nachas* (deep pleasure). This I promised. Oh, how I longed to see and hug my dear mother, father, sister, and brother. It would be soon, I hoped.

I explored the possibilities of calling home or somehow getting information to my family that all was well, that I was not dead, that I had escaped safely, and was waiting to get back to America.

"Max, I hereby officially notify you that this meeting is to determine a claim that you, while a prisoner of war, became a collaborator for and with the German army to the detriment of your fellow prisoners. What is your answer to this claim?"

I had been called into a conference at headquarters, escorted there by a security guard. The officer's announcement made me feel as if the sky had fallen upon me. I looked the captain straight in his eyes and in a calm voice said, "Sir, this is all bullshit. Do I have the right to ask who made such a libelous claim and when?"

"No, I'm sorry. We must protect the person or source of this charge against you. This charge cannot be treated lightly."

"If I had to give one guess who had filed such a lie, I would guess that it was a tall Polish GI who caused a lot of strife and ill will in our group. I literally had to pound some sense into him. I guess I was not wholly successful. At one point, after he wanted to fight me, I almost killed him. Now, I wonder if I should have completed that task."

"Max, for the record, our conversation is being duly recorded. Please tell me your side of the story. Start from the very beginning. We have several reports already of your conduct and leadership. We need your side of the story; your version of what really happened."

I did start from the very beginning, the Battle of the Bulge, December 16, 1944. I described the fighting, the wandering, and the havoc; the digging in on December 17 and the morning of the eighteenth; and my dead sergeant roommate, who died in my arms as tanks were coming up the hill and burying alive all the soldiers in the foxholes. I then related the moment when a dense morning fog fell over our area, allowing me to crawl out and scramble over the hill to the nearby woods.

I recounted the constant shelling and mortar fire and being knocked out by the concussion of an exploding 88 shell that killed a GI near me and covered me with his blood and guts.

I spoke about finding clothes and changing into them; of finally settling down in a German bunker on the old Siegfried line; and of the other American GIs in the pillbox and the coming of the German patrol—the SS troops—and our capture. In my mind, I was back in hell.

I continued to relate the rest of the story, talking for hours. When I came to the part where I became an interpreter for the German SS Panzer unit, they stopped me. The captain called in another officer, and they wanted me to give them the exact sequence of how and why I became the *Dolmetscher*.

"Why did you, a Jew, risk your life to give orders for everyone to get up? Didn't you realize that they could have also killed you on the spot?"

"Yes, I certainly thought of that but only for a very brief moment. The SS officer had already killed one of us and certainly would have killed more if we had not all gotten up. My feelings were really twofold. As a Jew, as part of my heritage, my soul should always be committed to helping my fellow man. The strange part, the reality of life, is that so many will not go out of their way to help save the lives of Jews. But also, I was a mess—I had dysentery, little sleep, little or no food, and was really pissed off at the bastard Krauts. I understood the German command to get up. I felt it was my inherent duty to get everyone up and keep them alive."

At this point, the captain put down his pen, looked at me, and said, "That was a brave act. I, personally, want to thank you. You undoubtedly saved lives. Please continue."

I told of leaving the front, the long "death march" for some, the signs at each village blaming the Jews for all their troubles, the end of the long march and boarding the railcars of death, arriving at the stalag, meeting the British POWs who ran the camp and their refusal to give us our own Red Cross parcels, and the transfer to our next home—the barn at Dobeln and the sugar factory.

I continued with the story of how the Russian prisoners gave up their one meal a day for the starving Americans, which seemed to rouse the attention of my two interrogators. I explained in depth the relationship that developed between us and the information I was able to learn about their operation prior to capture.

I was then told they had become aware of the actions of the British POWs, who ran some of the stalags and sold the parcels that belonged to all. The captain said to me, "Their day will soon come."

When I got to the part of my fight with the Polish SOB, they took special interest and had me repeat it again.

My tale continued with the attempts for the two failed escapes, the transfer to Linda, the meeting with Karl, and the final escape to the American lines.

I finished, exhausted and concerned.

There was a long pause, and the captain then said, "We have heard your story. It is my opinion you have told us the truth and were and are a brave person, well worthy of being an American soldier. We have also looked into the complaint file and have since found other soldiers from your group. They all spoke highly of your actions.

"Your story confirms the brief facts in this case, and I personally want to assure you that the unfounded allegations against you were certainly not warranted. We will not file any charges against the person who accused you—we have a lot more important things to do—but we will place this charge in his record. I believe that you have already taught him a lesson."

With that, the captain stood up, came to my side of the desk, raised his arm to his forehead, and said, "Max, I salute you! I am proud to have you on our side. Good luck and thanks ... and welcome back."

And so, with all that behind me, I was ready to get the good news that I was being transferred to a base camp near Paris to prepare for my being sent back to the States.

Our stay at the base camp was relatively short. Our trip back to the States depended on the availability of a troop ship—or in my case, a small "Liberty ship"—to arrive.

We had nothing to do but wait. I made friends with a young man who said he was going to go AWOL for two days. The chances were they might not even miss him. He wanted to see Paris. It was so close but yet so far. I decided to go with him. Who knew if we would ever get another chance to see Paris in our lifetime? I packed my duffel bag with all my belongings, including a German Luger and valuable souvenirs that I had accumulated. Most important of all, I had many pages of memos, with dates and thoughts of my life as a POW. These were the stories for my own healing and, when ready, if so lucky, to tell my children and grandchildren. I put a lock on my bag, marked my name all over it, placed the bag in a corner, and then Jim and I took off.

Leaving the base was no problem. We had no passes but just tagged along with a squad that was leaving the base on a field march. Once outside the base, we left the squad and headed in the opposite direction to Paris.

Hitching a ride was easy. We soon entered the outskirts of Paris and were in awe at the beauty of the city. Paris itself was never bombed. It was designated as a "safe city," not to be bombed or destroyed. The Germans had ruled Paris with an iron fist, but they recognized the merits of keeping it intact. After all, this was to become their city, a "German Paris."

The first thing we did was find the army finance building. We were able to draw two hundred dollars in cash, to be deducted from the monies due us—a cash advance. With money in my pocket and free as a bird, I felt like a king.

We were constantly approached by many Parisian women. Most were young and beautiful and some not so. They all wanted to show us a good time, and of course, there was a token fee attached to compensate them for their endeavors. I soon found out that Jim was quite experienced in these matters, but I was not. In disappointment, I said good-bye to Jim and took off on my own to discover the wonderment of Paris.

I was alone, happy, and thankful for all the blessings bestowed upon me.

Assuming the correct posture for an American soldier—stomach in, chest out, shoulders back, head high, eyes straight forward—I was so proud; proud to be an American GI as I walked the streets of Paris to my next adventure.

My long red beard was a visual reminder of my being a German POW, and I had not wanted to shave it off until now. There comes a time for everything, and now was the time to get rid of it. I walked and gaped at all the stores and merchandise being offered. There were many more female invitations, but I refused them. I soon came across a small barbershop and walked in. I explained as best as I could that I wanted a shampoo, haircut, and shave but made certain he understood that I wanted my mustache to remain, just trimmed and shaped. He understood. He was very good. One hour later, I walked out and emerged a new man. At the very least, I certainly looked different and was very pleased with the results.

For the rest of my stay in Paris, I was just content to walk, to look, and to take in the sights and sounds this great city offered. I was glad to be by myself just to think, to see, and to enjoy the moment in beautiful Paris. I vowed some day to return and once again feel the magnetism that this city offered. I rented a room in a small hotel, went out that evening, and had a great meal. I ordered cognac and a cigar and, in doing so, thought of Karl and the few nights in his loft. Never did the cognac and cigar seem as good as they had on those early mornings. Reminiscing and feeling a glow, the warmth of our friendship made the recollections so welcome. I missed him.

The next morning, I checked out of the hotel, did some more sightseeing, walked for miles on both sides of the river, and then headed out to the highway that would take me back to camp. It was a good thing, as my two-hundred-dollar draw was just about all spent.

I was a bit apprehensive as to what punishment awaited me for going AWOL, but I was prepared to face whatever they would give me. After all, I was already ahead of the game. I'd seen Paris and had a great two-day vacation. After what I had been through, I would have done the same thing over again. I was not concerned.

Upon arrival at the camp, I reentered without any problem. I went to my assigned barracks and was again met with bitter disappointment in my fellow GIs, my brothers-in-arms. They were up to their usual acts of self-degradation and stealing from one another. This was not the barn in Dobeln, where they stole bread. This was the last stop before going home, but still they stole and plundered. The lock on my duffel bag was broken open. My German Luger, helmet, insignias, and other memorabilia were stolen. I could have forgiven the bastards for stealing those valuable items, but they took all my pages of notes, dates, thoughts, and memories. Destroyed needlessly. I was heartbroken but soon realized that nothing had really changed. For the most part, they were not my kind of soldier, one that America could be proud of—a true all-American, typical Jack Armstrong image of young Americans. So be it. Screw 'em!

Our Liberty ship had arrived to take us back home, and final preparations were made for our going aboard. We were assigned quarters and again lectured on the safety measures while at sea. We were still at war, and there was still the danger of submarine attacks.

And so I gladly said adieu to France, to Belgium, to Germany, to all of Europe. I was going home, going back to my country, to my family, to my friends. Back to the Land of the Free. I felt pangs of sorrow, knowing that I was making the return trip while so many of my compatriots were left forever in this land, where they so gallantly had fought and died. What a price we had to pay. I hoped it was all worthwhile. I felt it was and was glad we'd fought a "war to end all wars." My brother, Sheldon, would not have to go to war.

Once aboard the Liberty ship, which was not built to be a troop carrier, we slept again in hammocks that, when full, held no more than about 250 soldiers. The hammocks, as on the trip over to England, were slung three or four high, and getting in and out of them was no easier. I thought my troubles and life-threatening experiences were over. Wrong! My hammock just happened to be in the bowels of the ship. Lucky me. There was no air conditioning, no fresh air, and no portholes. We again were just "human cargo" in a small cargo ship—destination: New Jersey.

The weather turned horrendous. This was good and bad. We were told that with such weather conditions, our chances of crossing the Atlantic without being attacked by German submarines were greatly improved. The German submarine fleet was still active, and their mission was to destroy troop carriers.

The Liberty ship was a small, mass-produced vessel to bring war materials to the European and African war fronts. It was not designed to compete with the Queen Mary for comfort or speed. Many of these small ships were torpedoed and sunk, and some just sank on their own, not able to withstand the stress of a large Atlantic storm.

The winds grew to almost hurricane force, with cold rain being driven by the wind, pounding mercilessly anyone and everything in its path. Eating a meal, for me, was almost impossible. I would just throw it up. My equilibrium and stomach were far from normal. I just gave up trying to eat solid food.

For two long, miserable days, our little ship fought the sea, the weather, and the headwinds unsuccessfully! We found ourselves blown back to France, from where we'd come. We were glad to see land and hoped to get off to stretch our land legs and get a hot meal without the effect of a bobbing boat. Unfortunately, we were not able to disembark. Being tied up at a port, however, lessened the effects of the hurricane.

Eventually, the storm let up, and once again we sailed west to America. The trip across took about three weeks. During that time, unable to stand the closed, crowded conditions below deck, I would stay on an upper deck. There, I tied myself to some hooks and spent most of the day just gazing out to sea or reading, when possible. Mainly, I thought about how I would spend my next few months, and I would plan for the next few years. There again is the old Jewish expression that my mother would often say: "Man plans and God laughs."

I was still sick, suffering from the effects of amoebic dysentery. I threw up almost daily, soon after eating, and would "dry heave" after that. Even though I was a mess, I was happy that this was the most serious of my war problems. Most wounded men would gladly have exchanged places with me. I was not complaining—just throwing up.

One day, while spending the day on the deck as usual, I got acquainted with a very nice young GI from Detroit, Michigan. His name was Wayne Mentier. Wayne was very pleasant-looking, of medium height— about five foot nine—slim and fit, with brown hair and a light complexion. He also couldn't stand being down in the hold and was glad to have company on the deck of the small, slow, bobbing ship as it plowed its way across the rough Atlantic.

Wayne told me his whole history and delighted in embellishing his love life, whenever the occasion permitted, with his girlfriend in Detroit. He was going steady with a girl named Shirley and couldn't wait to get back to her and to once again catch up. He asked me if I had a steady girlfriend. I told him that I was very fond of a young lady in Milwaukee, my barber's daughter, and her name also happened to be Shirley. We never got past the stage of holding hands. That, in itself, was already a step forward. Shirley and I communicated regularly while I was away and I, too, was most eager to resume our friendship upon my return.

Oh, how naïve I was in my early years. Things changed drastically in the next few months—but that's another story.

Wayne knew a lot of songs. He had a good voice and would sing as we passed the time on deck. I was *especially* intrigued with one song, and I had him sing it often. I eventually learned and remembered the words, and that song became a "trademark" for me later in life. I would get to sing it to my future wife and later to my three children and ten grandchildren.

"Always" became my theme song. More than that, it became my commitment, my devotion, and my pattern for my future way of life. What could be more idealistically pure as "I'll be loving you always, with a love that's true ... not for just an hour, not for just a day, not for just a year, but always."

Chapter Seven

Home and Healing

Time has a way of solving many problems. So it was. The terrible return voyage finally ended, and I promised myself I would never get on a boat again. But that, too, time solved, for I got to love taking cruises. What a wonderful way to enjoy life.

Upon arriving in New Jersey in July 1945, we were told we would not stay there long. We were to be processed, given medical examinations, and then sent to other bases around the country. It was in Paris, with the help of the USO, that a message was first sent to my mother and father that I was alive and would be coming home. What a great feeling that was. My mother was hysterical again but this time with the joy of actually being certain that her *zinnelle* (son) was well. I was finally able to talk to my family.

"Hello."

"Esther, this is your brother, Max." I heard a scream and a yell to my mother.

"Mom, come quick. It's Max."

I heard another scream, followed by Mother's crying as she picked up the phone.

"Momma, I'm home!"

"*Mein scheine kind* [my dear beautiful son]. I want to see you, to touch you, to kiss you. Where are you?"

"Momma, I'm back in America, in New Jersey, and I don't know how long I will be here."

"We don't care. We will come to see you, if only for a minute. Please find out when we can come and where. Please, I can't wait. I will go to the rabbi to tell him the good news. We will cry together! Esther, come and talk to your brother. Mark down all the information that he will tell you. We are going to see him. Esther, *schnell* [fast]!"

I explained to my sister that I would find out if there was enough time for them to come to New York and, if so, when and where we would meet.

I did get all the information and was able to get it back to the family. They were able to get a flight out to meet me for just a few days before I was shipped out again, this time to a VA hospital in San Antonio, Texas.

Our meeting was, to say the least, very emotional. My dear, beloved father couldn't hold back his tears, letting them flow freely down his rugged cheeks. We all kept hugging one another and asking the same questions over and over. I was brought current about the family and all our relatives. My little brother, now grown up and a handsome young man of fifteen, wanted me to tell him all about the war and my capture.

"Shel, come here and let me hug you again. All the stories will have to wait. There is too much to tell, and now is not the time or the place. Remember, you are the 'big son' now that I am not around. Promise to take good care of your mother and sister and listen to your dad."

"I promise, but you have to promise, too, that you will come back home soon, for good."

My dear mother kept repeating "*Zinnelle* [my son], please don't leave me again."

"Momma, I promise, never again, but it will be a while. You understand that, don't you?"

"Yes, my son, I understand. We will leave you. Remember, Rabbi Twerski wants to see you soon, too. He has been so good to us."

We had a nice meal, all of us together, and then the time came for our leaving. This time, however, it was a happy separation, unlike the last one when I was being shipped overseas.

Shortly after my family left to go back to Milwaukee, I was put onto a troop train for the long ride to San Antonio, Texas. It was apparent and true: *Join the Army and See the World*. My, oh my, there was so much to see, and San Antonio soon started a new, pleasant chapter in my life.

San Antonio is a very beautiful city. In 1945, it was not the large, metropolitan center that it is today. I was sent to the VA hospital and underwent a thorough physical examination that included tests and X-rays to determine the effects of amoebic dysentery, frozen feet, concussion, shell shock, starvation, and other war-related problems.

Life was a lot simpler in San Antonio, although I continued to throw up and was still shaken by my war memories of the thousands of dead soldiers, piled on both sides of a road. The smell stayed with me then, as it still is with me now.

Karl was always on my mind. We had had no further communication since our abrupt separation at the command center in Germany. I had no idea where Karl was, what had happened to him, or where to look to find him—impossible, it seemed, in the aftermath of the war. Germany was divided and in complete chaos.

I was notified that I was to get the Purple Heart and several other battle medals. It didn't impress me at all. I could have done without the war and without the medals, though I still feel the war was justified, as it stopped the German juggernaut from conquering the world.

One weekend, I attended a local USO dance. I was not a good dancer and really was still quite shy when meeting young ladies. I saw a beautiful young girl acting as a hostess and looked at her name tag. It read "Ann Rubin." After registering, she came up to me and asked if I would like to dance.

"Yes, but I don't want to look foolish and keep stepping on your toes."

"You don't have to worry. We all are amateur dancers, and my toes will be just fine."

With that, we did dance, more than once. She kept coming back to me during the evening, and we hit it off. She questioned me about my hometown, my family, and if I had a girlfriend back home. She tried to make me relaxed in her company. I noticed that she wore a necklace with a Jewish star. I then asked her about her family—did she live in San Antonio? She took me over to the bar and offered me a drink and another dance.

When it came time to leave, Ann gave me her telephone number and said, "I really enjoyed this evening and your company. If you would like, please call me. I would like that, and maybe we could take in a movie and later get a bite to eat."

"I want to thank you for being so attentive to a soldier who dances so poorly. You are very nice ... good to talk to and be with ... such a cute and intelligent lady. You made this a perfect evening. I will certainly give you a call, but I never know when I have some free time with the hospital schedule. I hate to leave now, but the last bus to the hospital leaves shortly. Thanks again."

"Don't worry about the bus. I have my car. Come—I'll drive you back to your base."

We arrived at the gate. I got out and walked over to Ann at the driver's side. I gave her a kiss good-bye and thanked her once again, promising to call her soon.

The next few weeks were filled with more medical exams and tests. I really had my fill of them, but I have to admit the VA was trying to do a very good job in treating the returning sick and wounded soldiers. Some of the wounded were in very bad shape. My problems seemed minor in comparison.

As my stay in San Antonio came to the end, I was called in for a medical review and conference, meeting with an elderly doctor of German heritage. He started by saying, "We have completed all the exams and find the amoebic dysentery can be an ongoing, long-time problem. However, we feel it is under control. As far as the problem with constant nausea and vomiting, that is a problem only you can cure."

Here he took off his glasses, looked at me, and said, "Max, you won't like or want to understand what I am about to tell you. We feel, due to the trauma of war and your confinement, many of your ongoing problems are symptoms of mental problems."

Hearing this, I was ready to get up and leave before I really lost my temper and my control. "You mean to tell me that when I vomit and have the dry heaves, it is all due to my being mentally deranged?"

"There you are, getting angry with me. Please, Max, relax for a minute. Take a deep breath and try to understand. The trauma you experienced, with all the death and the suffering, left its mark. This mark, these experiences, will eventually lessen but never disappear. As they lessen, so will your nausea symptoms. You must believe me. You are a bright young man who has undergone many traumatic experiences. Because of your nature and upbringing, these experiences left a toll on you. In reality, that is better than if they had no effect. You will live with your experiences, and with God's help, you may be blessed with a long and fruitful life."

I quieted down. I realized this kind, knowledgeable German doctor was telling me what he felt was the truth, and I believed him. I thanked him and promised to heed his valuable advice.

When I got up to leave, he also got up, came to me, gave me hug, and said, "Thank you for telling me about Karl. I personally consider it an honor to have known you. Good luck."

With that, I left this kind man—a doctor, whose advice I took and whom I fondly remembered for many years.

Knowing that I would soon be transferred to some other base, I wanted to see Ann again. That night, I took her to a nice restaurant. We had a lovely meal with several drinks, and when we came back to her house, we sat on the porch, as we had several times. She sat in my lap, and we necked. Ann clearly wanted to get married. A few weeks earlier, her father approached me with an offer. He told me if I should decide to marry his daughter, I would have a life of ease, with the wedding gift of one of his factories to call my own. The offer astounded me. I thanked him and told him that he had a lovely daughter, but the offer would not be the deciding factor in whether I would marry Ann. I was in San Antonio to get well, not to get married, and my first priority was to get back to Milwaukee to my family.

The next morning, I was officially discharged from the VA hospital and told I would be leaving that afternoon. I was to be transferred to ASF Camp Plauche, Louisiana, on the outskirts of New Orleans. Being transferred there was a welcome move for several reasons. It would tend to cool things down a bit with Ann, and I finally would get to see another beautiful, famous city. I had always wanted to visit New Orleans.

I called Ann and told her my departure was imminent. I thought that I was saying my final farewell. About an hour later, I was informed

I had a visitor at the main gate. Once again, saying good-bye was a hardship but in this instance, a necessity. I assured Ann that we would keep in touch, and I would send her my address as soon as I was given one. She cried and had me promise again.

Camp Plauche was located in New Orleans's Jefferson Parrish, away from the city's center that was hopping, alive, and vibrant. It served as a separation center for thousands of returning military personnel. You were separated from the service at the "convenience" of the government. In other words, there was no choice as to when you got discharged, unless you wished to sign up for another five years of army life. When finally discharged, you received your papers and a farewell. Then you were on your own to get back home or to go wherever you so desired. Quite a few men decided to stay in New Orleans.

Why was I sent to this separation center, instead of others closer to Milwaukee?

It seems the camp put out a request for a movie projection operator, for the movie house on the base. My record showed that I had such experience. I ran 16mm movie projectors for my high school, a far cry from the large 35mm projectors used in theaters.

After reporting to the camp and being assigned quarters, I went through another indoctrination, learning that the time for a discharge varied from a few weeks to "you name it." It all depended on getting your records assembled and determining your final payout. A sergeant instructed me to report to the movie theater for my work assignment, to see a certain sergeant who was in charge. I found the base theater and reported as directed.

"Who sent for you?" was the greeting I received. "We have three operators here who do very little work, if any. The hardest thing they have to do is scratch their ass. You are welcome to stay, but in reality, you'll be bored to death. See if they will assign you to another job."

I spent the rest of the day exploring the base. I came across the communication center where, after waiting my turn, I called home and told my mother the good news that I was up for discharge. Dad was at work, and my siblings were at school. After Mother stopped crying, she settled down, understanding that I would be coming home. I made her promise to make me her great potato latkes and *cutletten*.

One night while in the rec room, I met a sergeant who worked full time in the accounting department. He complained they were swamped with the task of updating records, for computing the payments due each soldier being discharged. He also mentioned they were short on capable people to get the job done. Since I had two years of accounting, I asked if I could be of any help. "Hell, yes," he said. "Just come to our office tomorrow. I'll have you meet the captain and the other guys, and we'll put you to work."

I looked forward to doing something—anything at all—that was meaningful.

That night, preparing for bed, there was a knock on my door. I opened the door to find Ann standing there, escorted by an MP. He said she was lost, looking for her husband. He left, and Ann threw her arms around me, kissing me. She said, "I'm here to stay with you, now and forever. Don't ever leave me again."

"Hold it. I'm still in the army, not a civilian. You can't come here to live with me. Under no circumstances will that or can that happen."

Ann calmed down when I assured her that everything would be all right. She told me she had found out where I was from a friend at the USO; she then packed a small bag, left home, and boarded the train to New Orleans.

"Do your parents know where you are?" Her answer was soon obvious—no!

I left my room, found a phone, and was able to reach Ann's father on his private line. I explained what had happened. They were very worried and were grateful that she was safe. He said he would arrange for a pilot to fly him to New Orleans, and he would be there as soon as possible.

"Mr. Rubin, I want to remind you that I promised not to take advantage of Ann. Rest assured that will be the case. She will be safe with me. I will await your arrival." I then gave him detailed instructions as to where to come.

Very early that morning, just as the dawn arrived, there was a knock on my door. I opened it and was greeted by Ann's father. He was accompanied by his pilot. They were there to pick up Ann and take her back home.

Upon seeing her father, Ann started to cry and was on the verge of becoming hysterical.

I assured her father that she was well and, eventually, she would understand that she could not stay with me or in New Orleans by herself. He had her collect her belongings, and with tears in her eyes, we said our farewells.

We promised to keep in touch. Several times, we spoke to each other on the phone. She sent me a lovely color portrait of her, but I never saw her again. I could only hope she was happily married with a houseful of lovely children and a husband who appreciated her.

I sometimes wonder what kind of life I would have had if I had married Ann. How would my life have changed, for better or worse?

My future was to be blessed with a beautiful, understanding, and devoted wife, Doris, and three gorgeous children. And they, in turn, blessed me with ten picture-perfect grandchildren. Now that is really a blessing.

My remaining days at the camp were spent organizing the department responsible for getting checks out to all those being discharged. This department was terribly disorganized. It took me a while, but I did get it to function like a business, instead of an overburdened government bureaucracy. By analyzing the bottlenecks created with the sudden increased demand for service, I was able to recommend changes to the captain. He, in turn, was smart enough to listen and put most of the suggestions into operation. The effect was a great reduction in the waiting time for checks and documents to be created. That, in turn, saved the government a lot of money, because they no longer had to pay soldiers for sitting around waiting for their final discharge.

I had made corporal some time ago. The captain called me aside and thanked me for my service to his department. He presented me with what he thought was a great offer. He would immediately give me sergeant stripes if I would sign up for only one more year.

I looked at him, had to smile, and said, "Several times I turned down the chance to become an officer. At this stage of the game, I really can't fathom becoming a sergeant. I thank you for the kind and generous offer but no—no way."

Finally, my turn came for separation from the military, to become just a plain American citizen.

On November 29, 1945, I received my discharge from the army and became a "free man" once again—free to leave, free to go home, free to start the next phase of my life.

Chapter Eight

A Civilian Again

I reached our house on Nineteenth Street and knocked on the door. I saw my mother, who gave a scream, rushed into my arms, and cried for happiness. I also had tears streaming down my face, as I gladly said, "Momma, I'm home."

The bus and train ride back to Milwaukee had been uncomfortable but also uneventful. Coming home, however, turned out to have one big surprise. There were always the same questions about the war, about being a POW, about escaping and, above all, about how much my family had suffered not knowing if I was alive or dead. But I found, now that I was among family and friends, that I did not want to talk about my war experiences—and I didn't. Some people resented my refusal and thought it a bit rude, but so be it. They all soon got the idea that I wanted to forget, and only in that way would I get some relief from the horrible memories that stayed with me, asleep or awake. I just was not able to dismiss the horrors of thousands of dead bodies and body parts, lying unburied and rotting, spewing out their obnoxious odors. As I looked at my mother, I was sorrowed, knowing that thousands of other mothers were unable to see their sons again. This is the true sorrow of war.

I just wanted to be part of a warm, loving family once again and to be left alone to treasure them. I kept looking at my parents, thankful I no longer had to worry about waking up as a captive and not remembering how my parents looked. Those memories still haunt me.

My mother was kept busy, cooking up a storm. She made all my favorite foods, and she made plenty, for the house was always full of relatives and friends who came over to see the "lost son." My mother was a great cook. The food always came out the same—delicious and perfect. However, if you asked her for the recipe, she couldn't be exact. It was always a little bit of this and a little bit of that mixed with TLC. Oh my, aren't Jewish mothers something, as all others are, to be loved and cherished and shown gratitude all the days they are with you.

Dad now had a partner, Abe Bookstaff, who also was a sheet-metal man. My sister's husband, Jack Spector, had joined my father's little firm. It still remained small, although there was a definite change in emphasis on wholesaling some of the roofing products that my father purchased for his own use.

Esther and Jack had moved into the lower flat on Nineteenth Street. I no longer had to sleep on the couch in the living room. I was able to share the bedroom with Shel, but we still could not close the bedroom door. The room was just too small.

I went to see Rabbi Twerski, a rabbi's rabbi. He was the leader of a significant percentage of the Jewish population in Milwaukee and was respected by gentiles as well. He was statuesque in appearance: tall, well-built, with deep facial features and a long, white, flowing beard. His eyes were large, dark, and penetrating. They saw into you and reflected the vast knowledge this man seemingly had on any subject that you would bring up. He looked like "Moshe Rabbeinu," as he reminded me of a picture of Moses. To me, he could have been the personification of God himself. That is how much I adored and admired that man.

When he saw me, he came to me with tears in his eyes. At first, he held me away from him and looked me up and down. Then he hugged and kissed me and said, "My many prayers to our Almighty, blessed be He, have been answered. I tried to write to you almost every day, not knowing if you were alive but hoping and praying. I do thank the Lord for listening to and fulfilling all our prayers—those of your parents, your many friends, your relatives, and of course, mine."

Life became routine. It was hard to grasp all those perils that I had faced during the war. Now the only danger facing me was the onslaught of well-meaning relatives and friends who wanted me to date and possibly marry their relatives or friends. Meeting young ladies was not a problem. It got to be a chore having to persuade some that I had no intention of getting married in the near future.

What was my future? I really was not certain.

I spent some time in my father's small business and rapidly decided that as much as I loved my father, I could not become a part of a small, four-employee company. That was not my future. How mistaken I was. Time and changing circumstances tended to shape my outlook.

Getting back to the University of Wisconsin School of Business was my first decision. The cost of my continuing education was covered by the GI Bill of Rights. The fee for a semester had mushroomed to the staggering sum of $139.

I was reunited with my dear friend, Phil Schneider. Phil had been wounded early in the war and was now fairly well recovered from the shrapnel wounds that had taken away part of his leg. My other close childhood friends—Sam Brazner, Larry Duckler, and Norman Eckstein—all returned safely from military life as well. Before the war, we had divided a silver dollar into four parts with the hope we would be able to make it whole again, if and when we returned.

Entering my junior year, I was required to have an interview with Professor Elwell, dean of the School of Business. I was in accounting but had to complete the last two years. Meeting with the dean was to be a mere formality.

"Mr. Gendelman, can you please tell me why you want to take the advanced courses?"

"I must respectfully ask you, Mr. Elwell, why you ask me to qualify my reasons to graduate from the School of Business with a degree in accounting. My grades were quite good. The only bad grade I received was in Logic. I got a C. To me, that was by far the most illogical course I have ever taken."

Mr. Elwell paused, deciding whether to give me an answer. He then said, "Well, let me put it to you this way. I feel there are *too many of you people* who want to be in my school with accounting as a major."

"Sir, can you please tell me what you mean by '*you people*'? Do you refer to poor people, white people, respectful people, or just a bias toward students who left the university for three or more years to fight your war—or, as I really surmise, are you referring to people whose religion is Jewish?"

"One must face facts. There are a certain percentage of Jewish people in Wisconsin, and when that percentage is exceeded by the entries to the accounting courses, it is my duty to level out the students in the courses."

"I fought for my country. I suffered horribly for my country. I helped save you from the atrocities of war, and you have the utter gall to come up with such slimy shit as reasons for establishing quotas. Such reasons are just the continuance of the hatred for Jews. Let me tell you something. A German SS officer once told me that Milwaukee is a great German city. He was correct, to a point. He would have been very proud of you, for continuing his work and Hitler's philosophies. He said this just after killing an American.

"Hitler killed over six million Jews. That, along with your quotas, will never happen again. I can assure you, Mr. Elwell, it will never happen again. You have a choice. I and other Jewish students get approved, assuming they deserve it, or I will splash your remarks and true feelings in every newspaper in Wisconsin and insist that the chancellor relieve you of your duties."

A few days later, I was officially notified that I had been approved to enter the School of Business to get a degree in accounting.

The next four months passed quickly. I learned accounting and met lots of lovely young ladies but never got serious with any of them.

I returned to my family home in Milwaukee for the summer and had difficulty in getting accustomed to being constantly waited on. Many times when I awoke, I would see my mother sitting on the nearby bed, just looking at me, with tears in her eyes. She was so happy to have me home, close to her and safe.

By the end of August, I was eager to get back to the university to start my senior year. I moved to a very convenient house, the Chez House, at 919 University Avenue, right in the heart of the campus. From my window, I was able to see the dorm for young ladies who were enrolled in the School of Nursing. The view late at night was fantastic. Phil joined me in the move. We still took our meals at the Bornsteins.

I dated frequently. On one occasion, I returned with my date to her residence at Tower View, a deluxe dorm for young ladies. My date that night, Helen Cohen, had asked me out to a special party. When Helen went upstairs to her room to freshen up, I got to talking to a nice-looking, perky brunette who was down in the lobby on her assigned telephone duty.

I started to kid around with her by asking, "Are all pretty girls selected to do telephone duty?"

"Of course, and some not so pretty, like yours truly."

"Why do you say that? It's certainly not true."

"Well, I am really curious to hear what answer you would give me. I must warn you, however, that it will be taken very lightly."

"And what answer can I give you that would appeal to you?"

"Oh, that the gown I am wearing is gorgeous, and that my necklace with its large diamonds enhance the sparkle in my eyes." She was dressed in well-worn jeans with a tight-fitting blouse. She wore little if any jewelry and no apparent makeup.

"Gosh, I could see the brilliant sparkle in your eyes even before I noticed the large diamond necklace. Would I be out of place to ask if some eligible gentleman gave you that necklace?"

"You know, I have so many expensive gifts bestowed upon me that I simply can't remember which suitor gave me that necklace."

"I can see that all of them have good taste in women."

"Do you always flirt with girls while your date is freshening up?"

With a provocative smile on my face, I said, "Well, true, I am with Helen, but this is the first time and possibly the last. I don't believe in dating just for the fun of it, unless there is a good reason to do so."

"And what reason could that be?"

"Why don't we go out on a date, and we could see if any good reasons come to the fore."

"Helen will not like to hear that."

"I've already told Helen. We will be just friends but not serious dating friends."

"I really have a hard time going along with such an arrangement."

"You are an open-minded young lady. Why don't we get together to discuss such arrangements in detail? Would you please do me the honor of having dinner with me on Wednesday, December 18? That is a special day in my life, and I would like to spend that day with a lovely girl. How about it? Please share it with me."

"What is so special about that day, December 18?"

"I can't tell you now; it's too long a story. But when we go out, I promise you will learn my story. This is such an important day in my life."

"You are very persuasive. I haven't even asked you for your name—or you for mine."

"A rose by any name is just as sweet."

"Come now, enough. What is your name?"

"No, really. My name is Max Gendelman. You can remember the name. You see a gentleman is not always a Gendelman, but a Gendelman is always a gentleman. This I will always promise. And what is your name, princess?"

"Doris Neubauer."

"And where do you come from?"

"Montclair, New Jersey."

"Gosh, I heard about Montclair. They are all 'fat cats' there."

"Yes, I'm sure there are some, but I am certain that is not the case with the Neubauers."

"What does your father do?"

"My father, David, is a carpenter. He builds homes."

"Now I know that we have a lot in common. My father's name is also David, and he also works on homes, putting on roofs, gutters, and sheet metal where needed."

"That truly is a coincidence."

"So now that we are so acquainted, please agree to dine with me on the eighteenth. Just say yes, so that I won't have to hound you."

"Okay, you get one night. No commitment for any more. Do you agree?"

"Sure, why not? I love challenges."

"What time, and how should I dress?"

"Let's make it very informal. We will go to my favorite restaurant, the Hoffman House, for great steaks. As for dress, you can go just the way you are or in anything else that you would prefer. You may wear as much or as little as you deem suitable. If I were given the choice, I would vote on the latter. In fact, the less you wear would be appreciated."

"Now, now, you are not nice. You sound like you have some plans in mind that I assure you will not be fulfilled."

"Let's leave the trend of this conversation. I can assure you that I always will be a gentleman whom you can trust."

"Fine, let's leave it with that. Wednesday will be fine. Thanks."

Helen came down, and we left to go to the Rathskeller for a beer and a brat. It was a typical swinging night in Madison. Later that evening, I felt it important to tell her that I had asked Doris out for a date. Her reaction was a bit unexpected.

"Great. She is a nice girl. She's smart, too, and works hard to be able to afford staying at Tower View. I don't know if she told you that she works weekends at Jimmie's Italian Restaurant. You should both hit it off and get to really know each other."

"Helen, I really didn't ask her out to taunt you. I really want to always be your friend—nothing more, nothing else."

"Max, I appreciate that but honestly, I've got too many friends. I'm in need of someone a lot closer."

The rest of the evening was a disaster. I took her back to the house and said good-bye. We never went out together again, although we remained casual friends.

Wednesday came. The day was greeted by a snowstorm. I did not think it advisable to take my car, as it didn't do very well on ice and snow. When I picked up Doris at six o'clock, I told her we would try to get a cab. The restaurant was about six blocks away.

"Why don't we walk? A short walk would do us both good. I have boots and a heavy coat. If I do get cold, you might want to keep me warm."

I was taken aback by her unexpected answer. It really threw me. Most of my other dates would never have suggested walking on snow-filled streets in mid-December.

"You sure?"

"Yep. I'll just put on my boots, and we'll be off."

The walk was great. The evening was not too cold. A light snow was falling, and Doris hooked her arm into mine, hugging me closer that way. We enjoyed the walk, looking forward to a great meal at a special restaurant.

In 1946, the Hoffman House was still a small, family-run establishment, later to become a much larger chain. We sat in a booth, sipped our wine and beer, and enjoyed the appetizers. The conversation was fast and witty—very enjoyable.

"Max, I've been patiently waiting for you to tell me why today, December 18, is such an important day in your life."

I started near the beginning, relating the different phases of my military life with my stay in England, enrollment in a sniper school, training as a sniper, deployment to France after D-Day to fight our way to Belgium and, finally, facing the Germans. I related my life as a sniper on the front lines, my problems with the cold and snow, living in foxholes or makeshift tents, and sleeping on the damp, cold ground. I continued with the start of the Battle of the Bulge, the initial force that first struck the area held by our company, Co. L of the 394th Regiment of the 99th Infantry Division. I recounted how the mother of all battles started at dawn on December 16, and I briefly described the next two days: escaping death after nearly being buried alive in a foxhole and living after being hit by an 88 shell. Then I told her how I was taken captive by SS troops on the eighteenth and kept on the front lines to bury the dead and their finally bulldozing thousands of dead soldiers to form hedges on both sides of a road. Everything I couldn't talk about since I arrived home came gushing forth. I wanted Doris to understand, as much as she was able, what I had experienced, as it was now a part of my identity.

Our dishes were served. We both ate in silence, enjoying the tender steak and the heaps of onion rings. We topped off the meal by sharing a great pie.

Doris kept looking at me. She was not an exotic beauty, but she possessed an elegance and an air of sophistication that was readily apparent to all who got to know her. She had dark hair; deep brown, sparkling eyes; and a perfectly proportioned face. And as I saw her studying me, it seemed she had a different opinion of who I was, knowing some of what happened. Then she quietly said, "I'm so glad you are here, so glad you survived the war, and so glad you invited me out and told me a little of your amazing story. I am also glad that I got to know you." Saying that, she leaned over and gave me a very tender kiss—one that I would always remember and hold dear.

Among all the girls I was dating, at that moment I knew this young lady was one I would want to know better—probably for the rest of my life.

On Valentine's Day, February 1947, I gave Doris a Bulova watch. Hers had broken some time ago and was never repaired. At first, she did not want to accept such a gift. I told her that it really was not very expensive and that she really needed one. I insisted. She finally accepted, and I was duly rewarded with an extra-special kiss. Yes, life was great. Shortly afterward, we agreed to "go steady."

I worked long hours at my accounting courses, and Doris focused on her studies. She still worked her job at Jimmie's. We somehow arranged to see each other daily, if only for a brief moment. A quick snack at the Rathskellar, a chopped liver sandwich at Stanley's, or a movie next door was the most time we could spare on a weekend.

Spring came, and we had a two-week break from classes. Doris wanted to go back to Montclair. I surprised her with an offer to drive her home. I told her that I would like to meet her parents.

Her parents were glad to meet me, and they seemed pleased with their daughter's choice of a boyfriend. Their house was small, and I had offered to spend the night in a motel. They insisted I sleep in the living room on a portable bed. Her mother, Anna, was determined, however, that we not further our relationship in her home. She sat up all night in a chair, watching over me and, in so doing, protected her daughter. With her mother very soundly asleep, Doris came over to kiss me good night.

My final semester before graduation was filled with hard work. I often brought cheese and crackers for Doris to eat and share with her roommates while she studied for her courses and exams. We did manage to spend a few weekends away from the campus, pledging our love.

In June 1947, I gave Doris a beautiful diamond engagement ring. She loved it. With tears in both of our eyes, we pledged our ever-endearing and everlasting love, and we looked forward to our marriage.

On Columbus Day, October 12, 1947, Doris Neubauer became my wife. The music was "Always."

My future was far from clear. I had thoughts of the FBI that I had considered joining while I was finishing college. I also had several offers to join accounting firms at a very low starting salary, although after getting my CPA, the compensation would be a bit more respectable.

Father suddenly became very sick and couldn't work. He had severe back problems that affected his spine and limited his ability to walk. The doctors told him he must rest, stay off of his feet, and take heat treatments. He had a talk with me. He couldn't run the business until he got better. He worried that he might not have a business to go back to if his back problem lasted a long time. He asked me to do him a great favor and take his place. He wanted me to watch, learn, and keep him posted on a daily basis as to what was happening at his company, United Sheet Metal Works. How could a son refuse a sick father?

"Of course, Pa. I will stay and help run the business until you get better and send me away. Don't worry. Just get well. I'll check with you every night. I'll need your input; after all, you're still the boss, right?"

"I thank God for having given me such a good son."

"Wrong, Pa. It is I who thank God for having given me such a great father. I am truly the beneficiary of your love and business acumen."

I started working for Dad that very day.

I never left the company. I never joined the FBI. I did do some private tax and accounting work but never went for my CPA. I never joined an accounting firm, but that was life.

My first salary was set at sixty dollars per week, the same as my brother-in-law, Jack, earned. I didn't complain, as I thought I would not be there very long. But fate had a different plan. I became involved in expanding our customer base, adding new products where possible, and creating a brochure for mailing and a mini-catalog with prices. I changed the appearance of the entryway and showroom and ordered signs to tout our new name, Century Steel and Roofing Sales, which would later become the Century Hardware Corporation. We were on our way to becoming a legitimate wholesaler of building materials.

The time came when Doris and I were able to move into our first real home, above my parents in the duplex we'd built with a GI loan. We were kept busy, buying new furniture and furnishing the house. One night, Doris asked if we could go to a nice romantic restaurant. I gladly agreed, and we went to a popular steakhouse named the Casino. During dinner, Doris told me the news that she was pregnant. I was overjoyed, and in bending over to kiss her, I spilled the bottle of wine. It was wonderful news. Our family would soon be three.

Chapter Nine

Karl, At Last

December 1950

My dear Max,

We have not heard from each other for a long time, and I'll break the silence by writing you and your family a Merry Christmas and a very happy New Year. May all your wishes come true ... I am healthy and in good hope that everything might come out well as ever. My education at the medical school will be finished in 1951, and I still don't know whether to specialize in internal medicine or in surgery. I am afraid that the latter faculty will be of more use in the future. ... How are you, old Max? I'd be happy to have a line from you, and I wish the very best to you,

Love, your Ted

Did you ever hear from Nick Grano?
Best regards from my girlfriend, Ala.

(Karl, I would later discover, when writing to close friends signed his letters using his middle name Theodore, or Ted, which his childhood friends called him. He always was Karl to me.)

Christmas Day, December 25, 1950

Dear Karl—my friend,

Your letter arrived. It was so good to finally hear from you and to really know that you are well. There is so much that I want to know but namely, reassurance that you are safe and in good health. Your finishing medical school soon is truly great news. That made me very happy.

As for news on this end, I finished my two years at the University of Wisconsin—Madison and got my BA in accounting.

While at the university, I met and fell in love with a lovely young lady (four years younger), and we got married in October 1947. ... Started to help my father in his small business and never left. ...

Several months ago, my first child, Nina, was born. The sun rises and sets on this little beautiful bundle of joy. Several weeks ago, we moved into a home that I helped build with the assistance of my father-in-law, father, and friends. This home has an extra bedroom, and I officially extend to you the use of same for as long as you desire.

We would love to see you after you graduate. Visit the United States and your friend, Max. I am still on a budget but will gladly contribute some funds to bring you to America and to us in Milwaukee.

Please, let's keep in constant touch. Your pictures are great. I forgot how handsome you really are. You must have a hard time fighting off all the lovely young German co-eds. On second thought, don't fight too hard. Enjoy ... Enjoy!

Let me know how your family is doing—mother, father, grandmother, and all. Until the next letter, your friend who wishes to have you here.

> *Love, much love, Max*
> *I miss the cigars, cognac, and Grand-mother's snacks.*

June 1951

Dear Max,

Sorry for the long delay in writing. I've been very busy, studying for my final exams. I'm glad to say that I think I did well. I will be having graduation ceremonies in about a month and have to make plans as to what I will really be doing.

Pardon the short letter. More after I'm a doctor.

Love to Doris and "Little Nina."

> *As ever, forever, your friend,*
> *Karl*

September 1951

Dear Dr. Kirschner,

Now that you are a doctor and will be making plans for your internship at a hospital, please consider doing your internship in a hospital in the United States. I may be of some help in getting you that position, but I'm sure you can have your choice of which hospital and what part of the country you would like to intern in.

I will help you with some funds to help you decide to intern here. A check for $500 is herewith enclosed. If and when you make your decision—to come to the U.S. —I will be able to furnish tickets to come from New York to Milwaukee.

Please remember. This money is to be used only for your trip to New York and not to be spent on Ala or your other beautiful lady friends. By the way, what is the latest with Ala?

Until we meet again—hopefully soon,
Max

September 1951

Dear Banker Max,

Your kind and generous check will be put to good use. I have decided to intern at Mercy Hospital, in San Diego, California. I had several offers and chose San Diego, to be close to Uncle Felix in Mexico.

I am making final plans to come to America and to visit with you. Will advise when I will land in New York.

As for my spending the money on girls, I believe that they should all be rich, beautiful, and willing to spend their money in taking me out.

Ala and I had been very close. When we did see each other, we pledged our affection and sealed our promises with mutual satisfaction. However, when I informed her that I would be leaving Germany to go to America, she became hysterical and realized that our relationship probably was at an end. She was still active in opera, very busy, and I'm certain that she will meet some other young men—proper suitors—who would try to share her vivacious personality, kindness, and desire to make passionate love.

Looking forward to the day when we will soon meet again.

Your friend forever,
Karl

Dear Karl,

Thanks for your prompt answer and the great news of your coming to New York and visit with us. Not sure of exactly when you will be arriving, I have made the following arrangement. I again must apologize for supplying you only with bus transportation. There is a prepaid ticket awaiting your arrival. Go to the Greyhound Bus Terminal building, and they will give you the ticket to come to Chicago, where I will pick you up and take you to Milwaukee. You must call me, however, to let me know of your scheduled arrival in Chicago.

Hope that you remember what I look like. I, of course, have the picture of that handsome young doctor.

This will be the last correspondence by mail. Can't wait until I see you and give you a big welcome hug.

Max

I couldn't begin to express the relief I felt when I finally received that first letter from Karl. When I had inquired after I had come home, army personnel told me he had escaped from the American custody, his whereabouts were not known by the US military, and truthfully, they didn't care. For five years, I had no idea whether he was in good health or even alive. I thought of writing to his grandmother at the farm, but I decided against it. Both Linda and Freiberg were now part of East Germany. The mail was being censored, and I thought there was a risk of retribution against them. I did not want to take the chance. He told me later what had happened to him after we were separated.

At least three different officers, each one of a higher grade, interrogated me. I was waiting for General Eisenhower to be next, but he never showed. I was not overly worried but still on edge—and rightfully so. I kept repeating my story in great detail, which was true on all accounts. They kept referring to the statement that you gave to the officer when we first were taken for interrogation. Our stories meshed perfectly. Finally, they all agreed that I was not a "plant," a German spy. After that determination was reached, they treated me much nicer.

I was later taken to a field hospital. My wounds were trimmed and dressed. I was given shots, medicine, and pain pills. The hot shower and change of clothes issued to me did wonders for my morale. Shortly afterward, I was put on a troop carrier that was going west to Belgium. There I was to stay until the war ended with Germany and then with Japan. I was content but still anxious to be with my family. After Germany surrendered, security eased up a lot. I was able to mingle more with the Americans, enjoying a beer and conversation with some officers and enlisted men in their lounge.

Leaving Germany was always on my mind. I kept putting together various plans and scenarios as to how and when I would take off and leave this camp. Problem was, where to go and how to get there. I even thought of sneaking aboard one of the DC-3s that was sitting on the field to carry the English troops home. I soon realized that without any papers, I'd never get past a thorough interrogation. Max, remember, how I threw my papers out of the truck when the Americans picked us up. I thought it was so much fun, but you looked scared. I was so naïve. My hand was getting better though, and I kept asking myself the question, "What would Max do if he was here with me?" The logical answer was to try to get to Hamburg. I thought from there I might be able to board a ship and make my way to Mexico. I had Uncle Fritz's address in my wallet.

One day while exploring my barracks, where I still had to sleep on the floor, I came across a room filled with a large number of good Russian fur coats. I selected a man's coat, took it to the barracks, and was going to sleep on it. One of the other soldiers came up to me and said, "The sergeant wants to see you."

Something didn't seem right. I was immediately worried that there could be a change of heart, and they would revoke my freedom. Why did the sergeant want to see me? I decided that I would not give him the chance to explain. I had a small bag with a few cigars, toothbrush, shaver, and some money. I threw in what food I had and then took off. I couldn't go through the gate, for the guards would have questioned me. Instead, I went to the area where there were many soldiers roaming around. At the right moment, I threw the small bag over the eight-foot fence, quickly climbed over, and fell to the ground on the other side. I stayed flat on the ground, waiting to make sure that no guards or GIs had seen me. The coast seemed clear. I got up, picked up my bag, and started to walk again.

By now, the European war had ended, and here I was on foot, doing the same thing I had done with Max. I wasn't anywhere close to Hamburg, so I started walking back to the south of Germany. I also was thinking about going to medical school. The most pressing concern, however, was to get food and shelter. Since I had farm experience, I decided to travel to rural areas and find a farmer who needed some help. Most farms only had women working in the fields. The men were all drafted into the army. The first farmer that I met gladly hired me. I worked in his vineyard and had plenty of food and shelter. This farm was near the town of Würzburg, which was a university town. I rode a bike into town and found out the medical school would reopen in May 1946. I registered, was assured of acceptance, and then returned to my farm family to stay until May.

I took just one trip into East Germany—I had to see if my family had survived. There had been no communication with them since the day you and I left. And again, I was lucky to get to Linda and the farm. The farm buildings had pretty much been destroyed by the Russians, but everyone was alive and well. They were so glad to see me. I stayed only a few days; I related my experiences and gave them my address at the farm and my schedule for school. I hated to leave, but I did not want to spend too much time behind the Iron Curtain. The Germans and the Russians there were not my friends. If detained, and if they found out of my previous escape and friendship with the Americans, I probably would have been shot.

It seemed like home, arriving back to the farm near Würzburg. The mail began to arrive. Uncle Fritz started to regularly send me bags of coffee. I left the farm family and moved into Würzburg to go to the university. I rented a small room for fifty marks a month. I sold the bag of coffee for three hundred marks, and that gave me some income for food and lodging.

At the insistence of Uncle Fritz, I also took chemistry for the first two years. He insisted that the future in Mexico (when I would come to him) would be in opening up a chemical lab or paint plant. "Treating sick people will not make you a fortune." I listened to him but decided to become a doctor, a good doctor devoted to helping my fellow man.

I must tell you about an incident. I remembered you telling me about a fight you had with a big anti-Semitic Polish guy in the barn at Dobeln. I would not have paid much attention to a large, stern-looking guy, except for the fact that he had a very wrinkled nose. One night in the camp, I was having a beer with some others and overheard this jerk talking very loudly about his time spent in a sugar factory in Dobeln, where he had to take some shit from a Jewish son of a bitch. He embellished the story, making himself the hero. I knew the story and noticed he failed to mention the fact that you almost killed him in a fair fight.

My entire family was thrilled with the news that Karl was coming to the States. They had heard my many stories about him. Now, they would be able to see him for themselves.

It had been six long years since Karl and I were last together. And now, with his arrival so near, time seemed to stand still, heightening my anxiety. He finally landed in New York, picked up his ticket, and phoned me with his time of arrival in Chicago.

On the day that I was to pick up Karl, I left home, driving my new DeSoto. It was a nice day. The rain had stopped the night before. All seemed perfect for his arrival. Having adequate time, I traveled at the posted speed limit on Highway 43 and then on I-75 to Chicago.

Close to the Illinois border, I noticed a police car with flashing lights in back of me. I knew that I was not speeding. I pulled over to the side of the road and awaited the officer, a sheriff, who approached my vehicle. I rolled down the window to hear him say, "Are you Mr. Gendelman?"

"Yes!"

"I have some bad news for you. Your wife has been in touch with the police and sheriff departments. You must go back to Milwaukee. The friend you were to meet was in a terrible bus accident."

I thanked the officer and turned back at the next turnoff. I was in a complete daze. I had so many questions that I knew would remain unanswered until I returned home and talked to Doris. I could do nothing except give a prayer that Karl was well.

Upon arriving back home, Doris greeted me with the quick assurance that Karl would be fine. She showed me the message that she received from a hospital where Karl was taken after the bus accident on the Pennsylvania Turnpike. Karl had a broken foot and arm and multiple bruises but nothing life-threatening. He would be hospitalized for about a week.

I later checked the news reports and learned the facts regarding the accident on the first turnpike in the United States. The Greyhound bus was traveling to Chicago from New York City. While the bus driver drove carefully at posted speeds, the rain and the darkness hampered his vision. Unbeknownst to the driver, there was a disabled semi-trailer truck, carrying long lengths of I-beams, in the road ahead. The steel beams protruded a distance past the rear end of the trailer, but the ends of the beams, marked only by some red flags, could not be seen at night in the rain. The disabled trailer had no lights or flares to display to oncoming traffic.

Karl was seated in the lower level of the bus, third row, aisle seat. He was seated next to a young man who also had recently arrived from Europe.

During the trip, the young man's friend, who was seated in the upper level, kept coming down to talk to him. It got to be a bit disturbing, as Karl really wanted to take a nap. Finally, after the third trip, Karl said, "Would you like to exchange seats? You can sit next to your friend, and I will gladly sit where you are."

"Wonderful, if you don't mind moving."

Karl picked up his few belongings. He was then escorted several rows up to the second level. He got settled in and hoped to be able to relax and get some sleep.

How wrong he was.

The misty rain continued. The roads were wet and slippery. The bus approached a curve. The driver suddenly saw the stalled semi-trailer with no lights directly in front of him. In desperation, he slammed on the brakes and said a prayer. The distance before collision was too short. There was the screeching of brakes, as the bus plowed into the long I-beams, which telescoped deeply into the bus.

The driver and six passengers were killed immediately. Karl was injured and knocked unconscious. He awoke with people screaming and utter chaos all around. In his lap was part of the head of the man with whom he had just recently switched places. By all rights, if he'd stayed in his original seat, he would have been killed. Instead, he was only severely injured. Once again, he walked away from death. Someone up above was still looking after him.

The sharp pain kept coming, never letting up. Being a doctor, Karl knew what the damage was. He might go into shock, but he knew he would survive this "crash landing."

Soon, there were many flashing lights and police cars on both sides of the highway. Ambulances were pulling up to the damaged bus—a vehicle that became the chariot of death for at least seven people; seven who were here one moment and gone the next. People with torches cut away the tangled steel, trying to create a pathway to get to the wounded and dying.

Chaos was everywhere.

It seemed like ages, but before long, enough of the steel was removed to allow the medics to enter and start removing the wounded and dead. Gradually, the wounded were loaded onto stretchers, placed into waiting ambulances, and then rushed to the nearest hospital.

I called the hospital and told them I would try to get someone to come to the hospital—or would come myself. We felt a sense of relief in knowing that although Karl was injured, he had survived. After being told where the hospital was located, I saw it was about eighty miles from Euclid, Ohio, where Nick Grano was living.

Nick owed me a favor—more than a favor, he owed me a marker. I needed his help to go see Karl in the hospital, to help with whatever documents were required, and to see what assistance Karl might need in getting back to me.

Over the past few years, there really was not very much I knew about Nick's life. I tried several times to communicate with him through telephone calls, Christmas cards, etc., but the effort was always one-way. Nick had married, had two children, and was happily living as a mason.

I finally reached Nick and explained the reason for my call.

"Max, I'm sorry that Karl is hurt. You caught me at a very bad time. We are having a family party, and I'm sorry but I just can't get away to see Karl."

"Nick, I really need you to go there now. See what Karl's requirements are and make final arrangements for Karl to get to me in Milwaukee. I will pay for any required charges."

"Sorry, buddy, can't do. I would any other time but not now." I was quiet long enough for Nick to say, "Max, are you still there?"

"Yes, Nick. I was just remembering that when I finally agreed to take you with us, I told you two things. If you caused a problem, I would kill you. The second thing I told you was that if we made it, you would owe me a marker. Some occasion might arise when I would need to call your marker. Nick, I'm calling it now! The decision is yours. But if you refuse, you will have to watch your back from this day forward. You will never know when you will see me or a third party or just feel the zing of a sniper's shot. That will be payment for a marker. One pledged and one refused. *Capisce?*"

There was a long pause, and Nick said, "Max, please give me a few moment's time. I want to talk to my father about going with me to see Karl. You are absolutely right. I never should have even thought of refusing. Please, please, pardon me. You and Karl were very good to me. I will do everything you asked. I'll call you back within fifteen minutes."

I gave him my phone number and thanked him. I told him I would be waiting for his call.

Shortly afterward, Nick did call. "I talked to my father. He will go along with me. We will leave tomorrow morning. When we get there and find out what has to be done, I'll call you."

"Nick, thanks. Your marker is fulfilled. Just to make you feel at ease, I can assure you that I would never have hurt you."

"I feel better now that you told me. I really didn't think that you would have. 'Til tomorrow, *adios, señor.*"

Nick and his father did leave in the morning. The rain still continued in that area. While en route, they were in an auto accident. Fortunately, they were not injured, although his father's car needed major cosmetic work. They rented a vehicle and finally arrived at the hospital.

That afternoon, Nick called. "Karl was surprised to see us. I was so glad that I came. Considering his injuries, he is doing okay. I left detailed instructions with him and the hospital. When approved for discharge, they will put him on the bus to Chicago. His same ticket will be honored. The hospital will contact you with the time of arrival. Is there anything else that I can do?"

"Nick, you did just fine. Thank your dad for me. I'm so glad you came with us out of Linda. Go home now; you must be exhausted … and promise no more auto accidents."

Nick was never a social person. His world was his immediate family and his work. That was his life. I later invited him to come to visit with us in Milwaukee. He declined. I regret that we later lost contact. I never saw Nick again.

I picked Karl up in Chicago. He was helped into the car, broken leg and all, and we headed for home.

Our front door swung open; Karl was greeted by my very pregnant wife, who was about to give birth to our second daughter, Lisbeth Amy. They hugged and kissed and tears of happiness were shed. "Little Nina" and Pal, our dog, had their turn in showing our guest that he was so very welcome.

That night, many relatives came over to meet the famous Karl Kirschner, the German officer who had escaped with their Max. My dear mother hugged and kissed him. She kept holding his hand and telling him how much she owed him for escaping with her *zinnelle*. Karl kept telling her—and many others that night—that it was really Max who had saved him from being captured by the Russians.

Karl, in their eyes as well as in mine, was the hero. He was there to be honored and adored and loved in a Jewish home, from his own so far away. We all were now his family, to love and adore him, as a son should be treated.

The company finally left. I had a barbeque and cooked a batch of tasty ribs. Karl and I settled around the fireplace, with Nina and Pal sitting and watching our welcome guest.

Doris later put Nina to bed and said good night.

Karl settled into his lounge chair near the fireplace. A fire was crackling, sending warm messages to both of us. A perfect setting for having a cognac and munching on some "nasheries" that Doris had prepared. We should have smoked a good cigar, like old times, but that would have to wait for later, when outside. (Cigar smoke made Doris ill, and all smoking was prohibited in the house.)

"Karl, I need you to tell me more about your life. I really know so little. What are your clearest memories?"

You might say I survived as a student. I chose to become a doctor and started at the university. That was, however, not my first choice. I would have preferred to follow in the footsteps of my Uncle Fritz, to be free, to roam the wild open spaces, to have a ranch, and to see the world. Uncle Fritz had written to my father many times to send me out of Germany. He was certain that there would be another war, and I should be safe with him. My father did not agree. How right Uncle was, and how wrong my father was.

I guess if Mother would have left her mother, we all would have gone to Uncle Fritz. That was really a no-brainer, for my mother would never have left. Her mother would have been left all alone, without her daughter to rely on and share the duties. She worked hard, even though knowing that she would be left out of the farm's ownership. She really was working for the benefit of her brother, as the owner of the property then had to pass it on to the eldest son. This law was called "ahrp galeek." Ahrp means to inherit, and galeek means the law.

I loved my grandmother, though. She ran everything. In addition to the farm, she had the right to sell beer and operate a restaurant. So she also had a dance hall, where beer and food were sold in the restaurant—the Rathskeller. She did so many things that, even now, many farmers' wives don't know or do. She made her own butter, cheese, and bread. She canned all the vegetables, cooked most of the meals, wove cloth, and did much more. When the restaurant was open, Saturdays and Sundays, she would sit past midnight until the last person left.

I remember there was a picture in the back of the restaurant, in the room called the Hinderstuhl, which meant the room behind the room that was usually used. The picture was of Hindenburg, a marshal and general in WWI, who became the second president of Germany. He had formed a party that was called "Stahlhelm," the Steel Helmet Guys. They were mostly war veterans who survived the war. These Stahlhelm members were very much opposed to the uprising of the New Man, who the people in our area called the "Mustard Men." The "Mustard Men" were the start of the Nazi Party, a derogatory term because of the brown color of the Nazi Party's uniform. Everyone would say "hier kommen die senfhosen," or "here come the mustard pants." There was much animosity. They were considered upstarts who were not going along with the large majority of people from the farm communities. The farm communities were comprised of people who generally were conservative in their thinking and desires. In the rural communities, farmers were noncommittal, but in each village, there were several Nazis who either became parvenus or burgermeisters (mayors). They would get the jobs and then rule the villagers. As I recall, however, the major politics were left to the larger cities. The farmers just acquiesced. They just wanted to be left alone. That, however, was not to be!

After my father was caught and stripped of his credentials for teaching Jewish students, he was forced to enter the German army. He was a reluctant soldier, an infantry officer. He had fought in WWI, as well as in WWII, and was wounded several times. He survived the Battle of Stalingrad in WWI by pulling himself aboard a horse-drawn sleigh in the snow, without a driver, and lying flat. The horse led him to safety, saving his life. In WWII, he won the Iron Cross by capturing fifteen Frenchmen single-handedly. He was on patrol at night, behind enemy lines. He came across a bunker and heard the soldiers speaking French, which he understood. Instead of tossing in a grenade and killing them, he ordered them, in French, to come out with their hands up and pretend to be part of a large squad of soldiers. When they got out, he marched them all back, not having to kill anyone.

Most of his later years, Father was not happy. He was doomed to spend his free days on my grandmother's farm, doing chores. He would rather have traveled like his colleagues. But since Mother had to stay and help Grandmother, he was not able to get away. I recall when he would take me on long walks through the hills and explain the names of the plants, the birds, the bees, and any animals that we would come across. Father instilled in me my first sense of medicine. For this, I was thankful.

In July 1943, my schooling was abruptly ended. My entire class was drafted. Most of us knew the war was over when Hitler invaded Russia, and America declared war on Germany. I had no choice. I was to become an of-

ficer in the German *Luftwaffe*. I chose the air force for many reasons. First of all, I liked to fly. I had taken training as a glider pilot while in our school summer sessions. Then I thought the training to become a fighter pilot would go on for about a year, and maybe the war would be over by then. Second, I didn't want to be caught down in the trenches like my father. If my end came, let it be in the air rather than in a trench. The navy didn't interest me, as I get seasick. Becoming a pilot would be interesting and, hopefully, I would get to spend some extra time away from the shooting.

Little did I know!

For my basic training, I was sent to a small French town, Onjere. This was right after the Americans broke through the lines at Senlo. We spent eight weeks there in boot camp, where we were taught basics, like shooting a gun. After completing the basics, I was sent back to Germany and started flight training. That part I enjoyed, as it was very exciting. I loved the thrill of flying and never thought I would be the one to be shot down.

My training as a pilot was such that you first train on a small double-winged plane. Those who are best-qualified continue on to become fighter pilots. They are the reckless and fearless ones. Then the next group is selected for the bombing aircraft. I was started on the older French Morane airplanes. I was trained to fly a fighter plane and as a copilot on the new jet aircraft invented and developed by the Germans.

The training as a pilot did not give you too much time to ponder the latest news. A lot of the very bad war news was kept out of the newspapers and off the air. The basic underground feeling among the men was that the war was just insane and created by men who probably were insane.

Our group was assigned flying duties to patrol Denmark, Holland, and the Baltic Sea. We were to spot enemy planes and Russian troop movements. We were mostly happy-go-lucky trainees and pilots, who lived and enjoyed each day as it came. We just wanted to stay alive and then go back to our previous life. We would fly out each morning, return to base, and then have two or three more missions that same day. While waiting, we would drink coffee, smoke cigarettes, and chat with the other pilots.

I kept hoping that the war would end with me alive to see Uncle Fritz, and roam his ranch, and feel free to make my own choices for my life. I would never allow a "Brown Shirt" to ever command me again.

Many of our group felt the same way I did. We couldn't confide in the officers, who were the elite group. It required special permission to even speak with them, but if I had to give a good guess, they also felt as we did.

And then it happened; I got wounded.

We were flying a mission of three airplanes and saw a truck caravan on a road with supplies. We had to know if they were Russian, so it was necessary to fly lower. If there were horses on the supply wagons, they were German. If fully mechanized, they were Russian. The Germans used horses because they were very short of fuel.

Russian tanks and artillery that were protecting the convoy started firing on us. I was wounded on my hand. Our group flew up and away to avoid more hits and headed back to base camp. The wound on my hand was not very serious but needed attention. The only attention I got was a bandage and tape put on an open jagged wound.

This was not my only problem. Our base was in danger of being over-run by Russian tanks. My squadron was to withdraw to another site in East Germany. Despite my wounded hand, I was still on active duty. In flying one of these Moranes, the left hand uses the throttle, whereas the right hand uses a stick. I was still able to fly fairly well.

After arriving at our new base in eastern Germany, we were assigned a task of flying around the area at sunset to make us familiar with the territory. I was the last plane to take off and decided that if I was ever to leave, it would be now or never. Being familiar with the area, which was fairly close to Linda and my grandmother's farm, I flew as near as I possibly could before I ran out of gas and had to crash-land the plane. We were not fully gassed up, for the mission was merely to fly around the base area. I was hoping I had not made a deadly error.

When I crash-landed the plane, although I was able to get out safely before there was an explosion, I now had several more injuries. There were multiple bruises and a deep cut on my left ankle that hit the bone. A piece of wood that had broken off upon crashing was imbedded very deeply in my left buttock. That was painful. I was able to pull out the jagged piece of wood and stuffed the hole with a scrap of cloth from my shirt to stop the bleeding.

Grandmother and safety were still about ten to twenty miles away. There was only one way to get there. I needed to start walking. I did, not knowing which troubled me more: the hand, the ankle, or the buttock. I really knew the answer. All three.

How I made it to the farm, I will never know. It was something that I will never forget. I had my left hand under my coat as a support, for it was so terribly swollen and infected. Grandma saw me walking (really, hobbling) up to the ranch house. She ran up to me and gave me a big hug and a squeeze. I could have gone through the roof. The hug was so painful. I guess I was close to passing out. She had no idea then that she had hurt me. She only knew how happy she was that I was back home, safe and sound.

Staying on the farm would have been ideal, but sooner or later, I would be forced to leave. I couldn't put my family in trouble. Besides, I was desperately in need of a hospital and real medical attention.

It was common for pilots to walk away from crashes and later show up at a base or seek a civilian medical facility for treatment. I decided to go to Linda and become an ambulatory patient. I felt I would not be in trouble then, for so many other pilots suffered injuries and walked away to get help but failed to report back to their bases. I felt that German officials would not be looking for me so soon. Many pilots had to leave their planes when their fuel ran out, and some were told to join retreating groups of soldiers.

They treated my wounds at the clinic as best they could, but in reality, it was horrible treatment. I was placed in a room with other wounded soldiers, who kept crying out for help. The proper help never came. Death did come, however, to many young men, who only wanted to live a peaceful life amongst their loved ones. I felt very depressed and knew that if I stayed there a long time, I too would get the "final solution."

When my mother and aunt, my mother's sister, came to visit, they took one look at me and at my surroundings and said, "My dear son, Karl. We are going to take you home and treat you ourselves. You will die here. Give us your few belongings. We will walk you out and hopefully, they will think we are just going for a walk with you. Our horse and wagon are not far away. Come, we must hurry."

My aunt actually took a picture of the hospital before we left. We were stopped once, but my mother explained that I needed some exercise and fresh air. Once away from the clinic, we were safe. With my family's love and the help of an old friend of the family, a retired doctor, I soon started to heal properly. Basic life improved for me, surrounded by a doting, caring family.

It was about this time that the army told Grandmother that they were taking over some of the farm for the purpose of holding prisoners of war. They would be kept there until the underground facilities in nearby Czechoslovakia were completed. In the meantime, she was required to furnish food and water when asked.

Several weeks after the fences and barbed wire enclosures were installed, the prisoners arrived. They were a dirty-looking group. Most of them probably had not showered in a long time. Showers were still not available for use at the new enclosed makeshift prison. We were told that most were American prisoners, and we were to stay away from them.

I spent a lot of time just walking on the farm and, in so doing, would walk near and around the fenced-in prison. During one of my many walks, I kept noticing a white, blond-haired, blue-eyed prisoner who generally always stood near the fence line. He would be closest to where the hay barn was, where I lived in the upper loft. After several days of seeing this prisoner, who looked like he could also be German, I decided to go up to the fence and talk to him.

"Karl, I drink to you. I thank the Almighty that you are here. You know how happy you make me to have you in my home. Let's drink, dear friend, to our friendship—for life. That said, now we can eat and drink like we did many years ago in your loft at the farm."

And so we toasted each other. I got up to stoke the fire. The hour became late, the fire had died down, and we decided to call it a night.

"Until tomorrow, my dear Max. Thank you for everything. Most of all, thank you for being my brother."

"Good night, Karl. Dream of your new life in America, surrounded by friends who love you. Dream also of all the beautiful girls that do! Sleep tight."

The next few days and weeks were spent in just making Karl feel at ease, not having to worry about money or travel arrangements. Many visitors came to meet our hero. The *Milwaukee Journal* had a reporter interview Karl and me. The interview became a front-page story.

I was still in a period where I was desperately trying to forget my experiences and the horrors of the war. I really wanted to forget but found that to be impossible. I was still reliving the "smell of death"—the smell of thousands of decaying corpses emitting their own "odor of revenge."

One evening, after Doris and Nina had gone to bed, Karl and I sat in easy chairs around a crackling fire. Pal had taken a liking to Karl and was cuddled up next to him. I brought out Grand Marnier cognac, and we relaxed, sharing our thoughts on what the future held.

"Karl, you haven't told me about Ala. There must be a lot to learn."

He laughed. A twinkle accentuated his deep blue eyes. "There is one problem. If I tell you all about this gorgeous young lady, you must promise not to run off to Germany and steal her from me. I'm only kidding, dear friend. You have lovely Doris. What more can a man ask for?"

I met Ala one night in Würzburg. She had the lead role in an opera and was a talented singer. I was given a ticket for the performance. When she appeared, it was like I was struck by lightning. She was so beautiful, with a figure to match. Picture this lovely creature with blonde hair, blue eyes, a pug nose, and clear complexion. She had a captivating smile and a voice to match. I sat spellbound throughout the entire performance. I knew I had to see her again—soon, that very night.

I explained to the guard on duty backstage that I had to see my cousin Ala. Not sure if he really believed me, but he let me go and directed me to her dressing room. I knocked on her door. An angel opened the door.

"Ala, you don't know me," I said. "My name is Karl Kirschner. I'm a medical student here in Würzburg. I saw your performance tonight, and you were magnificent. I knew immediately that I had to see more of you. Would you please allow me to take you out for a nice evening meal? I assure you I will do my best to make it a delightful evening. Besides, if you refuse me, I will be in a terrible state."

Ala looked at me in disbelief. Instead of refusing, she said, "You know, you've got quite a way about you. Yes, I'd like to have dinner with you. I hope I'm not making a mistake. Give me about fifteen minutes, and I'll meet you at the main entrance."

I was amazed and happy she accepted my invitation to dine that night. It was the beginning of a very warm and affectionate relationship. We seemed to mesh perfectly, hitting it off at the very start. We were each so different, but when together, we were one.

She traveled extensively with the opera during their season. When away, we managed to call and talk to each other. I called her in the morning, before classes, and she called after her performances. I was always up, studying and waiting for her call. She told all who tried to date her that she was to be married to a doctor after he graduated, and they were going to share the rest of their lives together.

Life seemed perfect—too perfect. Sometimes rain must fall and spoil your plans. With the good, there comes the bad. The opera season ended, and Ala was in town full time. She wanted to spend all day and all night with me. I tried for a while to see her as much as possible, but that was not enough. She wanted to move in with me. But in my small cubicle of a room, that would have been a disaster.

I still worked many nights and started to lose my ability to concentrate on my studies. My grades began to suffer, and shortly afterwards, my professor called me in for a conference. He knew of my relationship with Ala, and with as much tact as possible, he said, "Karl, you can be a great doctor or a great lover. At this stage in your studies, you will have to make your own decision. Which is the most important to you? Please, don't give up medicine. Graduation is not too many months away. Your future grades will tell me what your decision will be." At that, he got up and walked out. He was one smart German professor. I will always remember him and thank him for helping me see the right path for me to take.

I had a heart-to-heart talk with Ala and explained that if I were to become a doctor, I must stop seeing her so often, at all hours of the day. A lot of tears were shed, but she finally understood. We saw each other only when I felt my studies were caught up, and I could spare a few hours away from the books. My grades drastically improved.

But as you know by now, staying in Germany was not foremost in my mind. I was deeply disturbed by the Nazis and the willingness of the German population to follow Hitler so blindly. The carnage and atrocities, especially the slaughter of over six million Jews perpetrated by the regime, was inexcusable and will haunt Germany for many centuries.

No, I knew I must eventually leave Germany. That's when you finally heard from me, dear Max. I was hoping you would answer and somehow help me decide where to go and possibly assist me in that plan. I did want to come to America. In reality, any place away from the decadent German government would be an improvement.

Your mail and generous offer arrived. I was so happy. My mind and plans were now clear to me. I would apply for an internship as close to Mexico as possible and also get to see my buddy in the "good German city of Milwaukee." I showed the letter to Ala. She was silent for quite a spell. I knew that her anger was reaching a boiling point. She looked at me and asked, "Will you be making plans to go with me or without me?"

I told her I did not know yet if I would be able to go, and if so, with another person. I had so many questions that needed answers before I could give her a definite answer. Would I get accepted into an American hospital for my residency? Would I be able to afford the trip to America? How would I get situated? Would I have any free time as a resident? And when all that was settled and I was able to afford to bring her to America, would she even come to me?

"My home is here in Germany!" she yelled. "My future in opera is here. I grew up here, and I love it here. I always thought that I had a future here, together with you." She went on and on and finally said, "You are really one son of a bitch!"

What could I have done? She probably was right. She really was never in my final equation. I held her and tried to console her, but deep down, I knew that our relationship was over. She picked up her few belongings that she kept in my room, turned to look at me, and with tears in her eyes, opened the door and walked out. A part of me walked out with her, but that is life. I knew I'd never see her again.

"Karl, I'm sure you have set your first goal as finishing your residency and getting your license to practice medicine. As a single doctor, you will have to fight off lots of young ladies who would love to marry a handsome doctor. If you do marry an American woman, you also would become an American citizen."

"Yes, I am aware of that, but I want to assure you, that would not be the primary reason for my getting married. That would be a benefit, of course, for I really do want to become an American."

"Would that affect your relationship with your parents?"

"No! They are cooped up in East Germany. Each day is a torment for them. Hopefully, if I ever get settled, I will be able to bring them here to live out their remaining life in freedom."

"Great. Let's drink to the time when your parents can join you. Now I'm glad you are here with us."

Several weeks later, we all said good-bye to Karl, as he left to go to Mercy Hospital in San Diego, California. There, he would start his residency and his new life in a country that he would know and love for the rest of his life.

Chapter Ten

A New Life

Throughout the following decades, Karl and I would try to see each other as often as we could. On occasion, when his schedule would permit it, he would come to Milwaukee to meet the new addition to our family. Our third child, Bruce, was delivered in December 1954. But the greatest times were all the telephone conversations we had; several times a month, either Karl or I would make the call. He would keep me up-to-date on his life, as I did with mine. He would counsel me about my health, tell me to not push myself so hard with the business, and in turn, I seemed to be constantly advising him about financial matters. But mostly, it was enough just to hear the sound of each other's voice. Each conversation would end, without fail, with "I love you, my brother."

*

Max, my dear friend, leaving you, Doris, Little Nina, and Lisbeth, as well as your beautiful collie dog, is hard to do. You truly are the brother that I never had. I am grateful for your generous check of another $500. And I am keeping a record of what I owe, and someday I hope to repay you, not only for the money but also for all your kindness and friendship.

He traveled with one suitcase, as well as a smaller case that held his greatest treasure—a microscope that his uncle Fritz had given him. He told me the train ride had been comfortable and how excited he was that every mile was bringing him closer to his boyhood dream of "going West." He craved the large open spaces, the possibility of a ranch and cattle, and the room to roam, to think, and to be himself, like the life of his uncle Fritz, his idol.

When he told Mercy Hospital about his injuries and being temporarily handicapped, they told him someone would meet him at the train and escort him to the hospital. Upon arriving, he was greeted warmly not by one person but by a small group. They offered him a room at the hospital until he could manage to find his own living quarters. He gladly accepted. The hospital room, which was not being used for patients, was his first "home" in America.

He spent the next few weeks taking refresher courses, exploring the hospital, and assisting in whatever duties he was able to perform. He met the entire staff and was very impressed with the caliber of the personnel.

Finally, his cast was removed. He started the demanding schedule of medical duties of a resident intern on staff. That's when another young intern asked him if he would like to share the expense of renting a small apartment nearby. So Karl had his first temporary permanent address. He thought it was perfect.

He became a full-time resident doctor. He called and said, "I have no time to spend with the lovely nurses who give me the eye." But by the time fireworks were shot off on July 4, 1953, he had gotten a small increase in salary, seemed to enjoy a little more free time, and was able to pay more attention to the gorgeous young ladies working at the hospital.

So many important events took place in 1953:

> President Eisenhower was inaugurated.
> Stalin died.
> East Berliners rioted against Communist rule.
> Moscow announced the explosion of a hydrogen bomb.
> Tito became president of Yugoslavia.

But all those events seemed insignificant to the news that Karl delivered: he had met and fallen in love with a beautiful blonde, blue-eyed nurse named Dodie.

Karl met Dodie Herzog in August 1953. She was finishing up her nurse's training at Mercy Hospital. It took only a few dates for them to fall in love, and at Dodie's graduation ceremonies, Dodie introduced Karl to her Mother Superior as well as to her parents. All seemed to readily approve of him.

Karl was kept exceedingly busy at the hospital, preparing for his boards and his desire to specialize in pathology, but he took the time to write Dodie a love letter. She told me not so long ago, "After many readings of Karl's love letter, I couldn't help but believe that I truly was the chosen one. Probably very few women can truthfully say they've ever received such a tender letter of love. I had no idea what the future would bring, but in that moment, that letter was mine to keep forever."

That evening Karl took her to a quiet, secluded restaurant. He said, "Dodie, you must know that I am madly in love with you. I am asking you to become my wife, to share our future together. Please say yes. You would make me very happy."

With tears rolling down her cheeks, she said, "Karl, of course, yes! I do love you, and I will be most honored and blessed to be your wife, for good or for bad, for rich or for poor, or for whatever the fates have in store for us, together and always as man and wife."

The one small hurdle was the fact that Dodie was a devout Catholic, and Karl was a Lutheran. But Karl responded without hesitation, "No problem, my love. I certainly have thought of that. Most people in Germany are Lutheran. I've never been a devout church-goer. I will simply convert to your faith, Catholicism. This way, we can get married and exchange our vows in your church."

They were married in November 1953 in Dodie's church. They arranged the wedding so quickly that, with regret, Doris and I, with two small children and a blossoming business, weren't able to attend. The reception was not a large affair. Present were Dodie's immediate family, her friends from nursing school, and associates at the hospital.

After their wedding, she went to work for two surgeons, while Karl continued his residency in pathology at Mercy Hospital. He studied most every night for the California State Board examination, with his constant companion, a parakeet, at his side. Karl loved that bird. It kept him awake while he studied. During breaks from his reading, he taught it to say, "Stand back—I'm an eagle," and a few things that nice folk shouldn't repeat.

Dodie recalled, "One day my cousin Ruth came to visit me. She was extremely pregnant and did not see the bird sitting near Karl on the floor. Karl never forgave her for killing his beloved companion."

Their first two sons, Charles and Thomas, were born in 1956 and 1957. Karl and Dodie rented a small house for their budding family and were planning to remain in San Diego after Karl passed his boards. But then a young doctor named Tom McKeller, whom Karl had known at Mercy Hospital, asked Karl to visit him in San Luis Obispo (SLO).

When he and Dodie arrived in SLO, their first impression was that they were in the boondocks. Neither of them was impressed with the sparsely developed area. Cattle grazed on the oak-studded rolling hills. Karl's dream of open spaces had slowly been altered by the years he had spent in San Diego. Karl declined Tom's offer to join his practice, but Tom kept hounding Karl, continuing to beg him to reconsider. He finally agreed to move there only for a year or two. It was only a matter of time before he and Dodie fell in love with California's Central Coast. After a few years, there was never any question that they would ever leave the beautiful area. Their third son, Michael, was born in SLO in 1959.

Karl adored his sons and regretted later not spending enough time with them or with Dodie. He blamed himself. He told me, "I was so caught up in developing a practice and trying to be a great pathologist. I served quite a few hospitals in Central California. As they were small and did not have a doctor of pathology on staff, I purchased a small airplane and flew to all of them, being on call for patients undergoing surgery who required immediate decisions.

"Remember when I called you that I needed your advice? We met in Chicago. I told you the problem. I had a chance to buy a special machine that was just invented and now was being manufactured. These machines were capable of diagnosing blood samples with multiple tests and giving an analysis in a matter of minutes. Without this machine, it would take me days to get the answer back to the hospital. This could save lives, by giving a surgeon the answer while he is still operating.

"You told me I should definitely proceed with its purchase and asked if I needed assistance with financing. I remember telling you I could arrange payments over a thirty-six month period with the bank.

"When the machine was delivered, it became an instant success. I soon opened up a separate clinic for blood work and then purchased another new invention that was being promoted in Sweden. The aspiration needle allowed me to take a very minute sample of a suspected area to determine if it was cancerous or benign, replacing an intrusive biopsy, which could spread the cancer.

"My practice was very successful, but it came with a very high price. The pressure of my business started to weigh heavily on both Dodie and me. When I got home in the evenings, I started drinking scotch to bring me back down to reality. It was just too much of strain on our marriage. When Dodie divorced me, I really was heartbroken. I kept to myself. I still felt like a married man, certainly not a single man looking for female companions. I had my work and tried to see the boys more often."

In 1970, I used a business trip to Lompoc, California, as an excuse to go to San Luis Obispo to see Karl again. We met at his five-hundred-acre ranch. The road and entryway were such that it gave the ranch great security.

Upon arriving at the ranch house, I was met by a very beautiful woman. I was taken aback. She rushed up to me, gave me a big hug, a warm affectionate kiss, and said, "Finally, I get to meet Max. Do you realize that I firmly believe our Karl loves you even more than he loves me? I could and should be jealous, but knowing the story of your relationship, of your friendship, I can only say, please let me also share in his love for you."

Not only did her beauty startle me but also her exuberance and professed desire for friendship. She was, I soon found out, twenty-eight years younger than Karl. Sandra kissed me again, took my arm, and said, "Come—we must show you the Stenner Ranch. Karl and I love it here so much."

Karl took me for a brief tour. He showed me the various buildings and then the prized breed of British White Park cattle. What gorgeous animals. Back at the ranch house, we sat on his magnificent veranda, sipping beer. Sandra arrived with some small sandwiches to nibble on. Included were some small sausages. How appropriate! It took me back once again to his grandmother, who brought these tiny German wieners to Karl's loft in the barn at Linda.

Oh, how time seems to pass and silently creeps back again. Karl started to reminisce.

"I was always certain that I would leave Germany. After having come through the war alive, more through luck than my expertise, all the things that I hated about my country kept fueling my desire to leave. Many cities were totally ruined. Men just dragged themselves along, knowing that they had no future to look to. Yet the people who I always thought were the guilty ones, the ones we called *bonsons* [the big shots] were able to buy themselves clean. They could go down to the burgermeister and ask to be 'de-Nazified.' Money was exchanged, and just like that, they were clean to go back to their old jobs, although their beliefs seldom changed. Many were true Nazis; their beliefs were embedded in their minds and souls.

"Did I ever tell you, when I was in medical school at Würzburg, what my professor of surgery said? He liked me and said, 'You have a great future. After you graduate, you should work in the hospital and probably teach. I would like to invite you to do all these things as my assistant. However, there is one proviso. You must join our fraternity, *Esloggen Fraternit*. I will gladly sponsor you.'

"Max, *sloggen* means to strike someone. The history of German Burschenschaft [student associations] goes back to the time of Napoleon. One group would have to fence with swords the medical students of the other association. That is why you would see most German doctors with big *Schmiss* [dueling scars] on their faces and foreheads. Being thus wounded was a sign of virility and braveness. I kept thinking … I got through the war with some wounds but relatively minor ones. Why would I join such a group that was so alien to my way of thinking and living? It's true that the more things change, the more they stay the same. Germany was proof. It affirmed my need to leave a country that seemed to be headed right back into the old groove of a totalitarian state."

After coming to the States, Karl thought about how and when he could get his parents here. They were still living under extreme hardship in East Germany. His grandmother had died, which placed an even greater burden on his mother, who was running the restaurant as well as the farm. In 1959, he had arranged for a visa for them to come to San Luis Obispo. Seeing his mother and father made him so happy. Karl's boys loved their German grandfather who took them fishing. He told his parents that he would work out a plan for them to leave East Germany permanently.

A year or so later, he sent his parents money to sew into their clothing. The money was to be used after they left Germany. They were to take a trip to East Berlin on a train, as they had done before. This time, however, they would have no luggage. They would just have the clothes on their backs. When the train approached East Berlin, it always slowed down, and that's when they would jump off the train in the dark tunnel. They would then make proper contact with the people who would arrange for their departure from Berlin and Germany.

Miraculously, everything went according to Karl's plan. He had also arranged for prepaid tickets for his parents' eventual flight to San Francisco, where Karl and Dodie met them. They became citizens and lived in Morro Bay for the rest of their lives and are buried side by side in Cayucos, California.

Karl's mother told him many times before she died of how she would hide escaping Jews in her chicken shack and feed them. She knew her son had been saved by a Jew and felt she was repaying the kindness.

Karl told me the story of how he came to know Sandra. "One day, an elderly patient came to my office for a procedure. She was accompanied by her eighteen-year-old granddaughter, Sandra. As you can see, she is charming and extremely beautiful. Her grandmother, whom I had known for years, asked me for a favor.

"She said, 'Karl, please put my Sandra to work. She is very smart, can learn quickly, and will be of help to you. This way she will learn a profession. You don't have to pay her. I'm wealthy and will give her a weekly check. I want her to keep busy and to learn from a man whom I admire.'

"I told her, 'It so happens I am in need of a personal assistant. I will put your granddaughter to work. I will pay her, not you. If she works and wants to learn, I will keep her and teach her. If she turns out to be a poor assistant, I will let her go. Is that agreeable?'

"And so Sandra came to work—and work she did. She learned fast and soon was doing many of the blood tests by herself. I would always check each result but never found an error. It was nice having her do the work, and it was even nicer watching her as she did the work. She gave me some of the free time that I so desperately needed.

"As the weeks passed into months, I couldn't help but realize that Sandra was becoming quite attached to me. I started taking her out for dinner. She would hold my hand and forget to let go.

"Our relationship blossomed. The age difference bothered me but not Sandra. She kept telling me that true love knows no age difference. All my associates liked her. She then asked to move into the ranch with me. At first, I refused but later gave in.

"For Sandra's birthday, when she turned twenty-one, I took her on a trip to Sweden for the purpose of buying her a horse of her own. She had taken to riding horses at the ranch and had become very good. I bought her a Swedish Warmblood, which is a very beautiful, intelligent, purebred breed of horses. She named her horse Tribute. I instructed my ranch hands to build a large enclosed area for Sandra to ride her new horse. It was to be fully designed for dressage riding. When we returned, Sandra was absolutely thrilled with her own dressage riding facilities. She became an excellent rider, entered several major tournaments, and won some awards.

"Max, the days spent with Sandra have been happy. I'm content to keep our relationship at this stage, but she is always wondering when I will marry her. I just keep putting her off; I can't give her an answer. My love for Dodie and my boys is always present."

I called Karl to tell him of my new move to a place in the sun—Naples, Florida. We talked for a while and then he said, "Max, I really have to talk to you. Can we meet soon?"

"Sure, Karl, you name it—time and place."

"How about next weekend in Las Vegas?"

I wondered what was so pressing.

We met at the MGM Grand. We were both older, of course, but Karl still had a youthful outlook on life. His deep blue eyes still shined and gave the message that it was good to be alive.

"Karl, if it's okay with you, let's have a good meal, with a scotch to wash it down. The hotel dining room will do. I've got two tickets to a great show, Siegfried and Roy."

"As usual, Max, you are so efficient. This is just what I needed—a good, relaxing evening with you, just the two of us, like old times."

Later his story unfolded.

"I'll go back a bit. You know that I bought a very special horse for Sandra in Sweden. She named it Tribute and loved riding him several times a day. She practiced her dressage maneuvers and became very good in jumping and horse control. Her horse and her dog started to occupy most of her time. She gave up most of her duties at the clinic. Our evenings together generally ended up with her asking when we would get married. You know, I was very hesitant about getting married and entering a formal relationship with this beautiful, vivacious, young woman— a girl too many years younger than me. I did not worry about the next few years, but before long, I knew she would become tired of an 'old man.' I couldn't blame her if that occurred."

"But you always knew this. What changed?"

"You are correct. I did know, and I always felt that one morning I would change and get married to Sandra. That day never came. With each day that passed, Sandra and I seemed to drift apart.

"She had a dog trainer who also helped train Tribute. Ben was a handsome Israeli and came highly recommended to us. He was married to a blind woman, who lived in Los Angeles. Sandra and Ben spent many hours together each day, training Tribute and her dog. Training, talking, riding. He was a great listener to her problems, to her desires, and to her frustrations. He filled a need, one that Dodie also needed. I failed them both, being so busy and preoccupied with my mushrooming clientele.

"One day, returning to the ranch from the lab, I was greeted with a note from Sandra, which more or less said, 'Dear beloved Karl, I really love you too much to continue as we are. I am leaving you.' She wrote more than that, of course. She wrote how it was destroying her and that she believed it was also putting a strain on me. She wrote that I was her true love and that no one or thing would ever destroy the years of being with me. But that I had a wall around me that she just couldn't reach. And she asked me not to hate her."

As Karl told me this story, his eyes were moist and his voice reflected his sorrow. We took a small break, fixed some fresh drinks, and then he continued.

"Several years passed. I was lonely. I kept very busy with my practice—very busy. I really don't socialize very well. I'm a loner by nature and maybe by desire. I was bored by cocktail parties, where people stood for hours, drinking, and trying to be sociable. As a result, I was called less often to those affairs. That suited me fine. Deep down, I knew I was still in love with Dodie and my boys and was still reeling from the 'Sandra affair.' But that all suddenly changed with an urgent phone call. A doctor, a surgeon friend of mine, said he needed my immediate help.

"'Sure Bob,' I told him. 'What can I do for you? Just name it and consider it done.'

"Bob continued, 'Don't be too sure. You may turn me down. I hope not. This is urgent. I have a patient here who requires immediate surgery. This woman has a very large tumor that must be removed. If not, she will certainly die. I am willing to operate on her and do the extensive removal, but it is imperative that I know the state of the tumor when surgery begins. I need you to advise and assist me.'

"'No problem. Tell me when and where.'

"'Karl,' he said, 'there's one thing that you have to know. The patient is your old girlfriend, Sandra.'

"I was quiet for what seemed a long time and then I told him, 'Bob, tell me when you want me. I'll be there.'

"'I'm preparing for her surgery now. Please come as soon as you can.'

"We operated on Sandra. It was a long, delicate operation. Thankfully, the tumor was benign. Without surgery, Sandra would have died within weeks. She would now have a full recovery, but there would be a long period of recuperation. Regretfully, she will never be able to have children, but she should have a normal life expectancy.

"I soon found out that Sandra had no place to go. Her grandmother had died. Ben had left her penniless. Being the kind, old, foolish, sentimental man that I am, I offered her the use of a small rental home that I still owned.

"She said, 'Karl, fate has brought us back together again. They told me that you helped save my life. Thank you! And I accept your offer with no strings attached. Someday I hope to repay you for your kindness.'

"I told her to rest and get well. That would be repayment in full. She said she shouldn't ever have left me. She and Ben knew almost immediately that their relationship wasn't meant to be. He wanted to return to his blind wife in LA. They had run out of money, and after Ben left, she tried getting some jobs, working as a waitress and then in a clinic. When she got sick, she wasn't able to work or get around very well, but somehow she made it back to SLO with the intention of asking me if I would take Tribute and her dog if she died.

"She then said, 'Karl, will you please take care of Tribute? My dog can stay here with me.'

"Her recovery was slow. I paid all her bills and saw to it that she had everything she needed. When she was well enough, she came to the ranch to take care of her horse and eventually ride again.

"Our relationship never changed. She would ride on the ranch and then go back to her little home. I was content in keeping it that way. When she was fully recovered, she left me another note—this note."

> *Karl, I want to thank you for saving my life, for all the wonderful things that you have done for me, for your generosity, for taking care of Tribute, and for your past love. I will always love you. When I finally settle some place suitable for Tribute, I will send for him. Until then, take care and be happy. You deserve it. Love always. Sandra.*

We were both quiet for some time. Finally, I got up, took Karl by the shoulders, looked into his eyes, and said, "Karl, I believe it has all worked out for the best. You are still in love with Dodie. Your three boys are always on your mind. The Sandra chapter is over—a blessing. Just be happy with what you have; that is, a lovely, caring family; the ranch you always wanted to roam in; acclaim and respect from your fellow doctors and many patients; plus the love of your friend Max."

"Max, I needed to hear this from you. Thanks, many thanks for our everlasting friendship"

The next morning we both parted, wondering when we would get to see each other again. Two aged friends, one going to San Luis Obispo, California, and the other back to Naples, Florida.

Young Dr. Kirschner, early 1950s

Young businessman Max in front of Century Steel, 1947

Max and Doris's wedding, 1947

Karl recuperating in Milwaukee, 1952

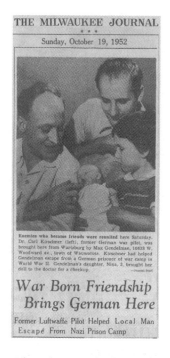

THE MILWAUKEE JOURNAL
* * *
Sunday, October 19, 1952

Enemies who became friends were reunited here Saturday. Dr. Carl Kirschner (left), former German war pilot, was brought here from Wurtzburg by Max Gendelman, 10638 W. Woodward av., town of Wauwatosa. Kirschner had helped Gendelman escape from a German prisoner of war camp in World War II. Gendelman's daughter, Nina, 3, brought her doll to the doctor for a checkup. —Journal Staff

War Born Friendship
Brings German Here

Former Luftwaffe Pilot Helped Local Man
Escape From Nazi Prison Camp

Headline, Milwaukee Journal, October 19, 1952

Karl and Dodie's wedding, 1953

Gendelman family, 1960

Phil Schneider with Max and Karl, 1976

Max and Karl at Bruce's wedding, 1976

Stenner Ranch, San Luis Obisbo, California, 1980s

November 2009

The Gendelman family, 2007

Karl's sons: Tom, Charles and Michael with their families, 2010 – 2013

Chapter Eleven

Milestones

Life became a routine that most people would gladly settle for, especially at the age of eighty-three.

Fall and winter seasons, about six months each, Doris and I spent in Naples, Florida. Spring and summer were in Milwaukee, where I spent almost my entire life, except for the three years when I was a guest of the government and given clothes, some meager spending money, and allowed to see Europe in all its splendor.

Having finally sold the family home on Seneca Road, we rented for several years when we spent the six months in Milwaukee. That was really not to my liking. I felt like a fish out of water, neither here nor there.

A new thirty-seven–floor high-rise was being built by a friend. It was connected to and on the shared land of the University Club of Wisconsin. The condos faced west toward Lake Michigan and north to view of the exultingly beautiful structure designed by the Spanish architect Santiago Calatrava. He became famous when he designed and built the signature Opera House on the shores in Sydney, Australia. One looks at our museum building with huge wings that open up—wings that are sails that seem to propel the building, like a large yacht, into the lake to start its journey. To me, it is a miracle of architecture and beauty.

We purchased a condo on the sixteenth floor and moved there in 2007. All our belongings from our family home had been in storage for several years. After two large truckloads were delivered, it took us a long time and a lot of work to finally settle in. In October, with everything in place, we left for our winter home in Naples. We felt good in knowing that when we returned in May, all would be in place, awaiting our arrival.

Several weeks after we arrived in Naples, we received an urgent message from the concierge in Milwaukee. It was difficult for him to give us the sad news that there had been a break in the hot water system on the nineteenth floor: *Your condo has been completely destroyed. All possessions are in storage. The condo has to be completely rebuilt. Please call!*

It took seven months for them to rebuild our condo, but we were able to restore almost everything. I have never gotten tired of spending some R&R time on our balcony, gazing at the lake and the museum, with its wings spread out as if it is about to fly.

My milestone of living to age eighty-five was celebrated with a gathering of the family at our Naples condo. I had prepared my well-known special barbeque recipes that always made my family thankful and look forward to the next one. It always consisted of ribs, chicken, baked bean casserole, fried potatoes mixed with sautéed onions, grilled Videlia sweet onions, and a vegetable platter of tomatoes, cucumbers, red and green sliced peppers, sweet corn on the cob, and kosher dill pickles. It all tasted great, washed down with a good beer or drinks of their choice.

My three children started by saying, "Dad, we are all here to ask a very special favor of you. We have abided by your wish that we not give you any special gifts. You told us that coming together as a family was the gift you wanted. We are here. We are giving you the gift you asked for. Now we have a request for you. We don't want your money. We want you and Mother to live a long time, at least to the age of 120. What we all want is for you to write a complete history of your war experiences and your life. We would like this, so we can tell all our children about their grandfather, and their children about their great-grandfather. We and they want to know the entire story. We have heard just a few of your experiences of meeting and escaping with Karl, but that is not enough. *Dad, you cannot refuse us—you must agree!*"

"With such an elegant appeal, who could refuse you, my beloved family? I do promise to start my memoirs and hopefully complete my story. I have been thinking of doing just what you have asked. In my mind, I will put down the story in simple words: the story of two soldiers, Max and Karl. I hereby state to you, one and all, that I will start my life's story and hope to finish it before I say good-bye."

I had to end my little speech there, for my voice was cracking and the tears of happiness were starting to flow. I'm such a softie where my family is concerned.

Later that evening, when all had left, I called Karl at his ranch. We brought each other current on all the family news. Karl told me that he had officially retired, closed his practice, and would be spending his days enjoying a quiet life at the ranch and with his family. He said that he had a little arthritis and an ache here and there, but considering his age, he couldn't complain. I told him of my plan to get started with our story and asked for his help in getting photos, letters, and general background history recorded for me.

As I pondered on how I could possibly start to put on sheets of paper the story of my life, how to capture my friendship with Karl, picking up the nuances in our connection that were felt more than expressed, I received a letter from the French ambassador to the United States. Each year the people of France honor selected Americans who merit recognition and special thanks of appreciation for their bravery, efforts, and accomplishments in fighting on French soil for the liberation of their country during WWII. And so on December 19, 2008, I was notified of the honor that the president of the French Republic had signed an official decree naming me *Chevalier of the Legion of Honor.*

The Legion Medal of Honor was presented to me and others at a ceremony held in Naples, Florida, on January 9, 2009. The medal was presented by a French general and a member of the French consulate. When presented, the very beautiful medal was pinned on my chest, and the general typically kissed me on both cheeks. It was very French, very formal, and very much appreciated.

I was very proud to have been selected for this honor and grateful to the people of France for the recognition, the honor, and the exquisite medal.

I was asked to give a few words. Unlike my own story that needed time to be put on the page, my gratitude poured out easily.

"My sincerest thanks to the people of France and to the Legion of Honor for bestowing this honor on me. I accept it in the name of all the Americans who fought for liberating France from the tentacles of the German armies. Many Americans fought and died in the effort to once again have France become a free nation.

"War is, in essence, a symbol of man's inhumanity to man. War is horror. Loss of freedom, however, is the greatest horror of them all. To live a free life in a free land, we must, at times, take up arms to protect that freedom. Cherish what we now have. Protect what freedom we have. War should be the very last solution. Thank you."

Chapter Twelve

November 2009

"Is this Mr. Gendelman?" a woman with a German accent asked. She was calling from San Luis Obispo to my home in Naples. It was November 11, 2009.

"Yes."

"This is Kirstin. I am Karl's housekeeper. We met some years ago when you came to the ranch. I have some very sad news to tell you. I am taking care of your friend, Dr. Kirschner. He is here at the ranch, bedridden and very ill. He is dying."

I was in a state of shock. I heard her words, but they didn't seem to register the very seriousness of the situation. These past few years, with both of us in our eighties, it had been harder for us to get together. My friend Karl was dying? I just couldn't fathom that.

"Please tell me, when did he get sick? What is his diagnosis? How imminent is his death?"

"The doctor has serious cancer. He was informed of it about three months ago. It did not seem so virulent then, but it suddenly started to spread very fast. He is now bedridden and doesn't get up anymore. Speech is difficult. We don't expect him to last much longer. I was hoping he would be with us for Christmas, but no." She was sobbing and tried to control her grief. "Chuck and Tom will be here shortly. Michael is at the hospital and will be here later this evening."

"Please have Chuck or Tom call me at this number as soon as they arrive. I want to talk with them and possibly have them arrange for a motel room. I will fly out tonight and will plan on seeing Karl tomorrow. I'll brief you as soon as I arrive, and we can see when I can be at the ranch."

"Mr. Gendelman, thank you for coming. He will want to see you before he dies. He always talks about his very best friend, Max."

"Of course. Please try to make him understand that I am coming, and he should hold on. I'll be there tomorrow."

I hung up and immediately called my son, Bruce, who was also close to Karl, having spent time with his boys during summer vacations. I reached Bruce at his home in Palm Beach. After he heard the sad news, he immediately said, "Dad, I'm canceling all my appointments. I want to go with you to see Karl. After we hang up, I will arrange for air tickets. I will call you back shortly."

Shortly afterwards, he had tickets to LA and a short flight on another carrier to SLO. He informed me that his youngest son, Daniel, then in New York, would fly to LA and meet up with us there. He had to see Karl once again, too. The Gendelman family would be well represented. Too bad it was at such a sad occasion. Bruce said that he had talked to Chuck and Tom several times. All arrangements were made.

I packed a small bag, grabbed a copy of my book in progress, and had Doris drive me to the airport. I kissed her good-bye and shortly afterward was on my way to Atlanta to meet up with Bruce for our flight to LA. Although I brought a book to read, I never read it. I kept seeing Karl and remembering him as a young handsome officer, as a dedicated doctor who had just gotten his credentials and passed his board, and as a romantic suitor who captivated and married Dodie. All those memories and many more continued to race through my mind, forming a collage of pictures of my dear friend. They were pictures that are burned into my memory, to stay there as long as my memory exists.

I met up with Bruce in Atlanta, and we went to our gate. Before long, first-class passengers were called. I had never flown first class, so getting a comfortable seat for the long flight was appreciated. It's good to have a son, especially one so brilliant and devoted as my son, Bruce.

Upon landing in LA, we found the flight to San Luis Obispo was full. Our only possibility was to fly to Santa Barbara, rent a car, and drive about one hundred miles to SLO. Bruce decided to do that and called

Chuck about our change in plans. He was given the name of our motel and detailed instructions on how to get there. When we arrived, Chuck and Tom would meet us for a light meal.

Daniel arrived from New York. What a wonderful grandson. What a handsome, soft-hearted, intelligent young man.

The long trip at night in a rented car was not to my liking. The road was quite narrow, often just two lanes and full of curves. Bruce was a capable driver, and we made the trip safely in about two hours. After checking in, we met Karl's sons. We went to a restaurant but left most of the food untouched. The time was spent in getting brought up-to-date. We talked about family and passed around pictures. Bruce showed Chuck and Tom pictures of his wife, Lori, and their four wonderful children.

The next morning, we were picked up to go to the ranch. So many memories jumped out at me as we neared the Stenner Creek Ranch, where Karl fulfilled his lifelong desire to be free and roam on lots of land, not cluttered with the remnants of an overcrowded civilization.

We turned off the highway onto a small dirt road that took us down toward a small creek. After crossing, we stopped to open a cattle gate, went through, closed the gate after us, and continued about a half mile over a bumpy, narrow path until we reached the fenced area and entrance to the ranch. It looked the same, but to me, it would never be the same. The ranch is Karl. Without him, it is just an expansive tract of five hundred acres.

Kirsten, Karl's housekeeper and nurse, greeted us warmly. She approached me and, with moist, tearful eyes, took my hand and thanked me for coming. I, in turn, pulled her close, hugged her, and gave her a kiss on the cheek. "My son, grandson, and I are here, of course, to see and say good-bye to our dear friend Karl but also to give thanks to you for being so kind and taking such good care of him. For all that you have done and for calling me, we are all so grateful."

"Mr. Gendelman, you must know that our Karl has not left his bed for the past four days. He has spoken very few words in all that time. Yesterday, I told him that Max was coming to see him and would be here the next morning. When he finally understood what I told him, he demanded that I get him out of bed, dress him, and sit him in his lounge chair to await your arrival. He said to me, 'Kirsten, our Max is coming. Now I will go in peace.' So you see, it is you that we thank. You have made all of us happy to have you here now."

With that greeting, we all walked into the living room, where Karl was sitting in his chair, awaiting our arrival.

Just one look at Karl, and I knew his days on earth were nearing an end. The family had hoped he would last until Christmas, but that was not to be. Christmas was over a month away.

I greeted him with a warm kiss on the cheek and a hug. His eyes told me that he was so appreciative of our coming.

Bruce sat on the stool at Karl's feet, took his hand, and said, "Karl, do you remember who I am? You gave me your most prized possession, your microscope. I still have it. It is now my prized possession. I see it every day in my home. Every day, I think of you and what you and my father mean to each other. The summer that I spent with you was—and is—a cherished highlight of my life. I have so many things to be thankful to you for. We love you. Good-bye. Good-bye, dear friend and hero."

With this farewell and with tears flowing down his cheeks, my dear, beloved son, Bruce, got up, and his son Daniel took his place on the stool in front of Karl.

"Doctor Karl, I am Daniel, Bruce's son. I really have known you all of my life. Your story and the story of my grandfather, whom we love dearly, are one and the same. Your lives are intertwined and woven together in a cloth, the memory of which I will wear and cherish forever. I hope that someday I may have children and grandchildren, so that I can tell them the story of my being here today and paying my last respects to you, a great friend not only to my grandfather but to all his descendants. Thank you for the great privilege of having known you."

With tears in his eyes, he just said, "Good-bye."

Chuck, Tom, Kirstin, and Grace, Tom's oldest daughter, were all present. Grace was very close to her grandfather, spending many hours a week with him, talking to him and caring for him. Grace was constantly in tears, hugging her father, Tom.

As I sat down on the footstool at Karl's feet, he seemed to gain strength. His eyes were clear and desperately searching to communicate with me. Suddenly, he spoke. He grabbed my arm and quietly said, "Maxie, Maxie you have come. You are here!" His voice gave out. He just continued to squeeze my hand.

I was silent for what seemed a long time. I kept holding Karl's hand and gently caressing it. I just did not see an old cancer-riddled man about to die. Instead, I saw Karl as he approached me on his grandmother's farm in Linda, Germany—Karl, a handsome young man with blond hair and blue eyes, statuesque in appearance, vibrant, with a magnetic personality that drew people to him. I saw a close friend whom I could count on my entire adult life. Karl once described us as two people who were fused like "steel and fire" to become stronger.

I brushed the tears away from his face, took both of his hands in mine and, trying to hide the sorrow in my voice, I said, "Karl, I am here to say a final good-bye between two close, old friends who have lived through adversity and happiness. Both of us have gone through a lot. I called you last month and asked how you were. The answer was always "fine." I understand that you didn't want to trouble me. You must understand, however, that when you hurt, so do I. Like twins that are joined together, our lives are closely entwined." I dabbed my eyes with a handkerchief and picked up a three-ring binder that held the first part of the book.

"I have here the beginning of the book that I told you I would be writing. Someday, the good Lord permitting, I will finish *A Tale of Two Soldiers—Max and Karl.* I needed to write this book, so that our children and their children can read and know and remember how a German officer and an America POW—a Jew—could have developed such a close lifelong friendship. Yes, a friendship that even death will not separate. Karl, my dear friend, look at me. Look deep into my eyes and tell me that you understand that you and I will be together forever in this world and, hopefully, in the next."

Karl nodded, and his eyes teared. He understood. His lips moved. His words were barely above a whisper, but they were clear, "Max, I love you."

I just sat there at Karl's feet, still holding his hands. Finally, I looked at Karl and said, "We won't let them forget our friendship and our love.

For time immemorial, we will be together like we are here today. One never knows what tomorrow will bring, but here and now and in the next world, we will be together. 'Til we meet again, rest, my dear friend. Rest in peace. Look for me, Karl. Maybe soon, maybe a little later. I'll come, Karl, and we will be together again."

With that, I had to get up. I was too choked to continue. The tears flowing down my cheeks were burning deeply into my soul. Everyone was very quiet. Bruce came up to me and hugged me. He didn't have to say anything.

The time came for us to be taken to their small airport to await our flight to LA. We had about an hour's wait. Tom and the children stayed with us the entire time. Laura, Tom's wife, came and to our surprise, she brought with her a person that I longed to see—Dodie.

Seeing her again was so wonderful. The years had been kind to Dodie. I always remembered her as a pert, vivacious, beautiful woman, full of life and love. Now, her blonde hair was shades of gray. She was still as beautiful as ever, with the twinkle in her deep, penetrating eyes that reinforced the magnetic attraction that drew you to her.

The memories just flowed out as if the container that held them had sprung a leak. They were such good memories. They were memories of Karl and Dodie in love; memories that time could not erase but embellished and polished to create the everlasting monuments of love and friendship that they both have always shared with me.

It was good to know that Dodie was happy and in control of her own life and had her family nearby.

We embraced each other. She expressed her thanks for our coming. When she saw Bruce, she ran up to him, hugged and kissed him, and commented on how handsome he was, just like when he spent a summer with them years ago. He was their "fourth son."

Later, we had a few moments alone. Dodie told me the complete story of Karl's illness. She saw him very often and spent some valuable time with him, just sitting, holding his hand, and trying to comfort him. They were together at the beginning. They would be together when his end came.

The flight was called. We said our good-byes. The children now had a new uncle. Tom and Laura had a new family. I kissed Dodie again, and we promised to keep in touch.

Doris greeted me with a kiss. She knew enough not to ask me about the trip. I just said, "Honey, I am emotionally exhausted. I am in need of a hot shower and some sleep. When I wake up, let's go to a nice restaurant and have a quiet night out, just the two of us."

Karl apologized all his life for the atrocities that his country did during the war and their slaughter of over six million Jews. He prohibited German from being spoken with his family. He loved being an American citizen. He felt God had given him a new life as well as a new country to live in. Things weren't always perfect—we never discussed politics; we had a tacit understanding that was off limits—but compared to the Germany he had known, America was magnificent.

Karl passed away on November 26, 2009.

And so, my story with Karl sadly ended. His death has left me sad and alone, another old soldier awaiting his time to come.

After

On August 14, 2011, my eighty-eighth birthday, I felt I had fulfilled the promise given to my beloved children three years before. I have written *A Tale of Two Soldiers*, with high hopes that my great-grandchildren and those of Karl's family will know of and remember the story of how two unlikely men—enemies—could meet and become lifelong friends. I wished that I could have written my memoirs as eloquently as some of my favorite authors. Not being a professional author, I apologize for my inadequacy. I have merely attempted to present my story as I saw it.

How does it feel to be eighty-eight? That is a question I have been frequently asked. After thinking about it for a brief time, the only answer that I was able to give was "I really don't know. You see, I've never been eighty-eight before."

The question that I ask myself is, "What do I expect and hope to occur in the uncertain time that I have left?"

- Keep my devoted, beloved wife—now of sixty-four years—in good health and provide for her when I am no longer around to take care of her.

- Keep my children and their families safe and healthy, enjoying life to the fullest.

- Allow me enough time to see more of my wonderful grandchildren get married, hopefully to one of their faith. If they all marry, then I'd have twenty grandchildren and who knows how many great-grandchildren. Wow—that's a family!

- As to world affairs, I have too many wishes and too many doubts for the nations of this world to solve their problems peacefully, hoping, however, that there never would be need for World War III.

I probably will never live to see the day when all nations will learn to live together in peace. One must hope that they learn, or their world—and all of ours—will also cease. This should never happen!

My dear parents and sister have left me. Their memories have never left.

My dearest friend, Karl, has left me.

War is a reminder of "man's inhumanity to man," but also it is a reminder of man's ability to care for each other.

Karl Kirschner
Born August 19, 1925, in Frieberg, Germany
Died November 26, 2009, in San Luis Obispo, California

Max Gendelman
Born August 15, 1923, in Milwaukee, Wisconsin
Died June 15, 2012, in Milwaukee, Wisconsin

Acknowledgments
from the family of Max Gendelman

Our thanks go to Lorna Owen for her patient and conscientious editing assistance. Lorna worked many long hours with Max via e-mail, holding his feet to the fire on details and patiently helping to craft this true memoir in his own voice.

We also would like to acknowledge Beth Hess and Launa Windsor, who worked with Max on early editions of the manuscript.

Betty Chrustowski provided encouragement and introductions. Leonid Strupinsky offered his wise counsel and energetic assistance. Photo image restoration was handled with artistry and sensitivity by Marc Tasman. We appreciate all of their efforts.

A special thank-you goes to the entire Kirschner family
for sharing their friendship.

Appendix A

Letter from the War Department Informing
Max Gendelman Is Missing in Action

al/ead

WAR DEPARTMENT
THE ADJUTANT GENERAL'S OFFICE
WASHINGTON 25, D. C.

IN REPLY REFER TO:

AG 201 Gendelman, Max
PC-N ETO 292

8 January 1945

Mrs. Fanny Gendelman
2461 North 19th Street
Milwaukee, Wisconsin

Dear Mrs. Gendelman:

This letter is to confirm my recent telegram in which you were regretfully informed that your son, Private First Class Max Gendelman, 36,807,750, Infantry, has been reported missing in action in Belgium since 18 December 1944.

I know that added distress is caused by failure to receive more information or details. Therefore, I wish to assure you that at any time additional information is received it will be transmitted to you without delay, and, if in the meantime no additional information is received, I will again communicate with you at the expiration of three months.

The term "missing in action" is used only to indicate that the whereabouts or status of an individual is not immediately known. It is not intended to convey the impression that the case is closed. I wish to emphasize that every effort is exerted continuously to clear up the status of our personnel. Under war conditions this is a difficult task as you must readily realize. Experience has shown that many persons reported missing in action are subsequently reported as prisoners of war, but as this information is furnished by countries with which we are at war, the War Department is helpless to expedite such reports.

The personal effects of an individual missing overseas are held by his unit for a period of time and are then sent to the Effects Quartermaster, Kansas City, Missouri, for disposition as designated by the soldier.

Permit me to extend to you my heartfelt sympathy during this period of uncertainty.

Sincerely yours,

J. A. ULIO
Major General
The Adjutant General

1 Inclosure
Bulletin of Information

Appendix B

Max Gendelman's First Letter Home
after Reaching the American Front Line

P.S. Don't write me till future notification.

AIR MAIL

May 8, 1945
Date of Escape
Date of Liberation
Date of War End

Dearest most beloved Mother, Father, Sheldon and my Esther & Jack

It is with tears in my eyes – for I am so happy – that I write this to my dearest lovely beloved parents and brother. I know you must have suffered with the uncertainty as to my welfare — whether I was dead or alive – safe or sound — but I assure you that I too had pangs of distress of not being able to let you know. But now I can assure you that I am well, happy, proud — yes proud to be an American & proud to be a free man, proud to be alive, and proud to be a son of such wonderful parents.

My story would take hundreds of pages to tell. I guess I'll leave that for later letters or when I can tell you in person.

Several days ago I made my third attempt to escape from the Germans. After walking close to 60 miles dressed as a civilian, we made the front lines. I saw some americans and started to run as fast as my aching feet could take me to them. The yanks wanted to give us everything they had, but a good

(2

American meal and now I write (20 minutes later)
a letter.

It was after our successful escape that we
were told by an officer that the war
ended tonight. Imagine what added joy
that wonderful news brought. After so
many years — it finally ended.

Dearest parents, I have prayed every
day (many times a day) that you have
had faith in our wonderful God and
stood up under the strain of the uncertainty
of my welfare. With God's help I shall
shortly be home. When I do I expect you
all to be in the very best of health, in
the highest of spirits, and really happy

Much must have happened since your
last letter of November '44. I hope that
I shall soon be on Uncle, that no casualties
occurred to members of our family — both in
and out of the service — and to my very dear
boy friends, especially Abe, Sam, Norm, & Phil.
There is so many volumes I want to write
and so many questions I want to ask.
That will have to wait.

In a few moments we shall be given a
shower, new clothes, and ———— more food.

AIR MAIL

Ah, food! I'm telling you, mom,
better polish up those cooking pots and
get even bigger ones, for I'm going
to eat you out of house and home.
Pop, get that business ready too, for
after a vacation I hope to jump into
it with you, —————— never to leave my
beloved family again.

It goes without saying that I send
my love, regards, and kisses to Baba Zaide,
Tante Chika, all my Uncles, Aunts, Cousins,
and friends.

Tonight I shall, if able, write another
letter and shall try to cable home.

Please, tell Rabbi Swerski of my welfare
and give him some token of my
appreciation.

    I have to leave now
        God Bless You
          Love and Kisses

            Marie

Notes

1. Prologue:
   Mortars coughed, rockets launched, 88s roared
   John Toland, *Battle: The Story of the Bulge*, p. 23.

2. Chapter Three: An Innocent Abroad
   A German machine gun killed our lieutenant, Charles M. Allen.
   George W. Neill, *Infantry Soldier*, p. 130.

3. Chapter Three: An Innocent Abroad
   ... called "Hitler's Secret Weapon."
   John Toland, *Battle: The Story of the Bulge*, p. 7.

4. Chapter Three: An Innocent Abroad
   German patrols coming toward us like ghosts ...
   George W. Neill, *Infantry Soldier*, p. 131.

5. Chapter Three: An Innocent Abroad
   Toward the northern end of the 99ᵗʰ, the German's 2ⁿᵈ Division ...
   John Toland, *Battle: The Story of the Bulge*, p. 7.

6. Chapter Three: An Innocent Abroad
   At midnight, the men of the 2ⁿᵈ Division ...
   John Toland, *Battle: The Story of the Bulge*, p. 7.

7. Chapter Three: An Innocent Abroad
   General Kriefe reported the Luftwaffe ...
   John Toland, *Battle: The Story of the Bulge*, p. 22.

8. Chapter Three: An Innocent Abroad
Five Panzer—German tank armor—divisions were to be withdrawn ...
John Toland, *Battle: The Story of the Bulge*, p. 14.

9. Chapter Three: An Innocent Abroad
... from Field Marshal Gerd von Rundstedt: Soldiers of the Western Front!
John Toland, *Battle: The Story of the Bulge*, p. 22.

10. Chapter Three: An Innocent Abroad
Suddenly the fog lifted like a theater curtain ...
John Toland, *Battle: The Story of the Bulge*, p. 99.

11. Chapter Six: Escape
I'll be loving you always ...
Music and lyrics by Irving Berlin, 1925.

12. After
... man's inhumanity to man ...
Robert Burns, "Man Was Made to Mourn: A Dirge" *Robert Burns: Selected Poems*, p. 54.

Select Bibliography

Blum, Howard. *The Brigade: An Epic Story of Vengeance, Salvation, and WWII*. New York: HarperCollins, 2001.

Burns, Robert. *Robert Burns: Selected Poems*. New York: Penguin Books, 1993.

Cavanagh, William C. C. *Dauntless—History of the 99th Division*. Dallas, TX: Taylor Publishing, 1994.

Goolrick, William K., Ogden Tanner, and the editors of Time-Life Books. *World War II: Battle of the Bulge*. New York: Time-Life Books, 1979.

Humphrey, Robert E. *Captain and Commanders (Volume 18) Once Upon a Time in War: The 99th Division in World War II*. Norman, OK: University of Oklahoma Press, 2008.

Neill, George W. *Infantry Soldier*. Norman, OK: University of Oklahoma Press, 2000.

Parker, Danny S. *Battle of the Bulge: Hitler's Ardennes Offensive, 1944–1945*. Boston, MA: Da Capo, 2001.

Toland, John. *Battle: The Story of the Bulge*. Lincoln, NE: Bison Books, 1999.

Wilson, George. *If You Survive: From Normandy to the Battle of the Bulge to the End of World War II, One American Officer's Riveting True Story*. New York: Ballantine Books, 1987.

About the Author

For fifty years, until the mid-1990s with the anniversary of the end of WWII, Max Gendelman had refused to talk about his wartime experiences as an assigned sniper in the 99th Infantry Division, Company L, 394th Regiment. Fighting on the front line of one of the war's deadliest battles, the Battle of the Bulge, he was taken prisoner. Born in Milwaukee, Wisconsin, in 1923, this young Jewish GI witnessed the horrific images that left him shell-shocked. He spent the next five decades trying to avoid the "painful memories." He poured all his energies into running the successful business he founded and headed, the Century Hardware Corporation, taking care of his family and nurturing the lifelong friendship he forged with the German Luftwaffe pilot who had helped him escape from the POW camp. He received the Purple Heart, among several medals; the Republic of France also awarded him with the title *Chevalier of the Legion of Honor*. Gendelman died June 15, 2012, one month after he finished the final draft of *A Tale of Two Soldiers*; he was buried with full military honors.